# theGREAT *Commission*

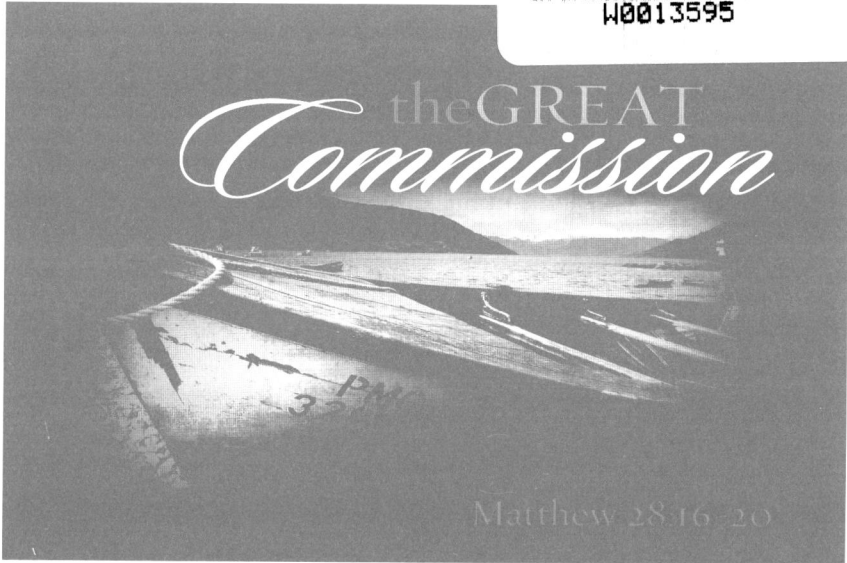

Matthew 28:16-20

# EVANGELISM GUIDE

# EVANGELISM GUIDE

## Steve A. Thomas

For All Occasions
High Wycombe, Buckinghamshire

Published by  For All Occasions, High Wycombe, Buckinghamshire, UK.

**Used by permission:**

Excerpts taken from Church Evangelism by  John Mark Terry c. 1997
Broadman &  Holman Publishers.

"**Reprinted by permission**. Rediscovering Pastoral Ministry: Shaping Contemporary ministry with Biblical Mandates, by John MacArthur and Master's
College Faculty, 1995, published Thomas Nelson Inc. Nashville, Tennesse. All
rights reserved."

Unless otherwise stated, all Scripture citation is from the Holy Bible,
New  King James Version, copyright © 1979, 1980, 1982
by Thomas Nelson, Inc.

**Library of Congress Cataloging-in-Publication Data**

Thomas,  Steve  A, 2009-
      Evangelism: The Evangelistic Guide for  Understanding Evangelistic
Outreach / Steve A. Thomas.
      p.  cm.
   Includes bibliographical references.
   ISBN 978-0-9562783-2-6
   1. Evangelisic work.  I.  Title.

*To Lurline*
*My wife, friend, and supporter-admirer.*
*To my lovely daughters, Christina and Stephanie.*

**And**

*To my colleague and friend in ministry, Eglan Brooks, who planted the idea of this guide. And to my churches, John MacArthur, and John Mark Terry, who made it possible for this guide, specifically for the members of the Seventh-day Adventist Churches, to be printed*

**Thank you**

# INTRODUCTION

# Introduction

It is becoming noticeable, especially in the United Kingdom that many of the laity are lacking in motivation for gospel work and have not been adequately trained for mission work. Members of many of our churches are not fully aware of the function and role of the body of Christ and are not sufficiently mobilized for the mission and ministry given by Jesus. Peter Wagner suggests, "a vital sign of a healthy church is a well-mobilized laity that has discovered, has developed and is using all the spiritual gifts for growth" (Wagner, The Healthy Church, 16.) He further writes that "Christians are to function as members of Christ's Body, and each person has been given a spiritual gift or gifts to do a certain job. Therefore, one of the most important spiritual exercises for a Christian is to discover, develop and use his or her spiritual gift" (Wagner 16.)

Once a congregation has acquired a suitable property as their place of worship, that congregation must now examine and plan for its future. Wagner reminds us "a vital sign of a healthy church is a church big enough to provide the range of services that meet the needs and expectations of its members. To be attractive to newcomers, a church has to serve its members well. If it does, it will in turn spread the news that the church is doing things that appeal to outsiders as well (Wagner 16.) Many congregations have never analyzed its community. But with the acquisition of a building came the realization that the church would have to "carefully examine the needs of the unchurched people around it, establish a philosophy of ministry that will meet those needs and plan to grow until it is large enough to conduct that sort of ministry adequately (Wagner 17.)

## Purpose of the Evangelistic Guide

The purpose of this guidebook is to help members to better understand the mission work of evangelism as well as to provide some guidelines for evangelistic teams during the pre-planning and planning stages of such events. In addition, it is hoped that the guide will become a tool in helping to develop strategies that will improve and strengthen the areas that are weak, while maintaining and strengthening those areas that are healthy.

One can see that over a number of years, some of the churches in the conferences have experienced growth, others have stagnated, and still others have declined. Among the churches experiencing an increase, in many cases the increase was limited to numerical growth, with very little expansion-taking place in other vital areas of church life.

It must be remembered that when growth is not matched by numerical increase in membership, then the result is insufficient resources, materials, insufficient people to train as leaders, not enough young people to carry the mission forward, and a lack of finance to reverse the stagnation or downward trend.
Because of the problems previously mentioned, an evangelism guide, for training existing leaders, was considered necessary to begin concentrating on improving the areas of need.

This evangelistic guide started with the Reading Central Seventh-day Adventist Church (RCSDA) as well as the Whitley Seventh-day Adventist Church (WSDA). Several resources, gathered over a number of years, were compiled and distributed during church board meetings as well as training sessions. The focus being to avoid paraphrasing other writers work, but rather to seek to reproduce them in a format that members could wrestle and debate with, rather than debating with the theological understanding of the compiler. Of greater importance was the inclusion of the writings of Ellen G. White, without much interpretation because of the danger of the reader questioning the compiler's interpretation. It is believed that the fact that many of the laity do not have access to all the resources at the disposal of many of the ministers of religion, the guide would seek to bridge that gap.

In addition, the Personal Ministries Department director, of the British Union Conference of Seventh-day Adventists, also requested such valuable materials should be made available for other Personal Ministries leaders.

Chapter 1 introduces the concept of evangelism and leadership role and responsibility. Here, I've reprinted, with permission, sections from the outstanding work of John F MacArthur and the Master Faculty work from one of my favourite books on Pastoral Ministry (J. F. MacArthur., Master Faculty, 1995, 305.)

Chapter 2 begins with a look at planning the campaign as outlined in the book Evangelism. I have included some of the inspirational work of Ellen G. White, which is second to none (White, Evangelism).

Chapter 3 examines evangelistic sermons and provides some guidelines for the evangelistic team. Here, I have cited some of the work from one of Jamaica's evangelist, Pastor Burnett Robinson, as well as the writings of Ellen White.

Chapter 4 outlines and describes bible study approaches as well as how to prepare a bible study. Here, I cite work from the General Conference of Seventh-day Adventists Lay Activities Department as well as Ellen White.

Chapter 5 describes the restructuring necessary in order to allow the mission of the church to become number one again. Here, I have reprint some of my previous work from my doctoral dissertation on strategic planning.

Chapter 6 highlights some aspect of effective church planting, from the point of view of a missiologist. His work is reprinted, with permission, to avoid any dispute with the compiler's point of view on the subject.

Chapter 7 provides information on preparing the church for evangelistic meetings, while chapter 8 looks at making disciples. Chapter 9 gives some sample organizational charts for restructuring the church. While chapter 10 and 11 highlights some of the well established job descriptions for those planning an evangelistic series as well as how to lead people to Christ.

It is not the purpose of this guide to explore all the methods, theories of church growth or other forms of evangelism. The purpose is to provide an evangelism guide in one easily accessible manual, as opposed to having many books and manuals. While there are other excellent ideas within the realm of outreach, the guide attempts to stay as close as possible to that which is found in the writings of Ellen White.

The following are used in this guide:

**Activity Schedule**: A Gantt chart describes the activity schedule, timing, sequence, and duration of project activities. The activity schedule also includes the milestones used for monitoring progress and the assignment of responsibility for the achievement of those milestones (European Commission 69.)

**Core values:** A church's primary values derived from the Bible that drives its ministry (Aubrey Malphurs, Value-driven Leadership, 14.)

**Evaluation:** A periodic assessment of the efficiency, effectiveness, impact, sustainability, and relevance of a project in the context of stated objectives (European Commission 69.)

**Gantt Chart**: A method of presenting information graphically, often used for an activity schedule (Ibid.)

**Goals:** The ultimate results that the project seeks to accomplish. All projects are goal-directed. The overall goals of a non-profit organization are usually described in terms of its mission, or purpose (McNamara, Field Guide to Nonprofit Program, 6.)

**Impact:** The effect of the project on its wider environment and its contribution to the wider objectives.

**Monitoring:** The systematic and continuous collecting, analyzing, and using of information for the purpose of management control and decision-making.

**Objectives:** Description of the aim of a project or program. In its generic sense it refers to activities, results, project purpose, overall objectives, and goals.

**Outcomes:** The impacts on the people affected by the project.

**Output:** The tangible results produced by the programs.

**Programmes:** Related and well-organized resources and methods intended to provide certain related products and/or services to a group of constituents (McNamara 148.)

**Project Purpose:** The central objectives of the project in terms of sustainable benefits to be delivered to the project beneficiaries.

**Resource Schedules:** The project budget that contains a list of items, costs, and quantities necessary for the project to be viable (European Commission 73.)

**Results:** The outputs produced by undertaking a series of activities. The results are what the project will have achieved by its completion date (Ibid.)

**Small Group:** An intentional, face-to-face gathering of three to twelve people with a common purpose of discovering biblical truth.

**Strategic Planning:** The way to identify and move toward desired future states. It is the process of developing and implementing plans to reach goals and objectives. Christian is to discover, develop and use his or her spiritual gift" (Wagner 16.)

# CHURCH EVANGELISM

# 1

# CHURCH EVANGELISM

It is said that successful church evangelism of any type includes a systematically planned approach to growth. That it requires taking the gospel commission to "go into all the world" and applying it to each member's family, neighbours, coworkers and friends.

J. F MacArthur, Jr., R. Mayhue, and R. L. Thomas, said

> Ministering in the church constitutes the highest privilege. Nothing could be more honourable or have greater eternal significance than serving our Christ in His church. This privilege is also the most serious responsibility a person can undertake. Fulfilling this privilege and discharging this responsibility demands a comprehension of the church and its ministries that is correct according to God's Word. Understanding those truths is the foundation of effective ministry. Unless spiritual men devoted to these realities lead the church, the next generation of churches will not be without blemish. (MacArthur et al., 1995)

Some contemporary church leaders see themselves as pastoral businessmen, media figures, pulpit-entertainers, psychologists, philosophers, or pastor of laws. Those notions contrast sharply with the tenor of the symbolism Scripture employs to depict spiritual leaders.

In 2 Timothy 2, for example, Paul uses seven different metaphors to describe the rigors of leadership. He pictures the minister as a teacher (v. 2), a soldier (v. 3), an athlete (v. 5), a farmer

EVANGELISING

(v. 6), a **workman** (v. 15), a **vessel** (vv. 20–21), and a **slave** (v. 24). All such images evoke ideas of sacrifice, labour, service, and hardship. They speak eloquently of the complex and varied responsibilities of spiritual leadership. Not one of them makes leadership out to be glamorous.

That is because it is not supposed to be glamorous. Leadership in the church—and I am speaking of every facet of spiritual leadership, not just the pastor's role—is not a mantle of status to be conferred. It is not earned by seniority, purchased with money, or inherited through family ties. It does not necessarily fall to those who are successful in business or finance. It is not doled out on the basis of intelligence or talent. Its requirements are a blameless character, spiritual maturity, and above all, a willingness to serve humbly.

**Jesus' metaphor** for spiritual leadership, one He often used to describe Himself, was that of **a shepherd**—a person who tends God's flock. Every church leader is a shepherd. The **word pastor** itself **means "shepherd."** It is appropriate imagery. A shepherd acquires new sheep (from the market place or biologically), leads, feeds, nurtures, comforts, corrects, and protects—responsibilities that belong to every leader, officers and members of God's church. This is certainly the aims and objectives of the church, for which evangelism is the core.

Please note that shepherds are without status. In most cultures, shepherds occupy the lower rungs of society's ladder, and are often thankless and unnoticed until the needs arises for a sacrificial lamb. That is fitting, for our Lord said, "Let him who is the greatest among you become as the youngest, and the leader as the servant" (Luke 22:26).

Under the plan God has ordained for the church, leadership is a position of humble, loving service. Church leadership is ministry (and minister is that which God gave in Matthew 28:19,20), not management. The calling of the ones whom God designates as leaders is not to a position of governing monarchs, but humble slaves; not slick celebrities, but labouring servants. Those who would lead God's people must above all exemplify sacrifice, devotion, submission, and lowliness.

Jesus Himself gave the pattern when He stooped to wash His disciples' feet, a task that was customarily done by the lowest of slaves (John 13). If the Lord of the universe would do that, no church leader has a right to think of himself or herself as a pastoral/officer elitist.

Shepherding animals is semiskilled labour. No colleges offer graduate degrees in shepherding. It is not that difficult a job; even a dog can learn to guard a flock of sheep. In biblical times, young boys—David, for example—herded sheep while the older men did tasks that required more skill and maturity.

Shepherding a spiritual flock is not so simple. It takes more than a wandering bumpkin to be a spiritual shepherd. The standards are high, the requirements hard to satisfy (1 Tim. 3:1–7). Not everyone can meet the qualifications, and of those who do, few seem to excel at the task. Spiritual shepherding demands a godly, gifted, multi-skilled man of integrity. Yet he must maintain the humble perspective and demeanor of a shepherd boy.

With the tremendous responsibilities of leading God's flock comes the potential for either great blessing or great judgment. Good leaders are doubly blessed (1 Tim. 5:17), and poor leaders are doubly chastened (v. 20), for "from everyone who has been given much shall much be required" (Luke 12:48). James 3:1 says, "Let not many of you become teachers, my brethren, knowing that as such we shall incur a stricter judgment."

Therefore, as you read this evangelistic guide, remember that the focus is first to recapture the purpose of our mission as a witnessing community. The things that should motivate us for service, and then follow them. I believe that a clearer understanding of evangelism, as given to us by the servant of

EVANGELISING

the Lord, Ellen White, will correct anyone on the pathway of self-centred evangelism and the mixing of spiritless outreach principles with God given methods.

I have, therefore, attempted to compile some of the tried and tested approaches, guides and information learnt in the practical school of evangelism, while working with Pastors James Phillip, Richard Holder, Winsley Hector, K C Henry, and Eglan Brooks and the school of the prophet (Northern Caribbean University, formerly West Indies College). Thus the reader can catch a glimpse of the tried and tested pathway spoken by the prophet Jeremiah.

> Thus saith the LORD, Stand ye in the ways, and see, and ask for the old paths, where is the good way, and walk therein, and ye shall find rest for your souls. But they said, We will not walk therein (Jeremiah 6:16, KJV.)

Therefore, the purpose of this Evangelistic guide book is to provide an evangelism guide in one easily accessible manual, as opposed to having many books and manuals. In addition, it is hoped that the guide will help pastors, ministries leaders, and members to better understand the many faces of evangelism, as well as to stimulate a new drive towards fulfilling the mission and ministry given to us by God.

# EVANGELISING

*The function of the pastor is to lead the church in the attainment of this grand design, the worship of God (the first grand purpose of the church). Obviously, the minister himself must be a true worshiper of God. He must practice in a personal and authentic way the worship of God. Then he must assist the congregation in the worship of God by helping them to understand the New Testament aspects of worship for the believer and to lead in the corporate worship of God during the various gatherings of the Christian community. He must teach the church to worship, lead them in worship, and join them in worship.*

# 2

# EVANGELISING
## A Witnessing Community[1]

According to J. F. MacArthur, R. Mayhue & R. L. Thomas, "the function of the pastor is to lead the church in the attainment of this grand design, the worship of God," the first grand purpose of the church (305). The first Obvious point here, one that is presumed, is that "the minister himself must be a true worshiper of God" (Ibid). He, the pastor/minister,

> Must practice in a personal and authentic way the worship of God. Then he must assist the congregation in the worship of God by helping them to understand the New Testament aspects of worship for the believer and to lead in the corporate worship of God during the various gatherings of the Christian community. He must teach the church to worship, lead them in worship, and join them in worship" (306).

MacArthur said that "it is not unusual to view the second and third grand purposes of the church as extensions of the first. Witnessing and ministering to one another are in a sense individual acts of worship." Therefore, two more ways to worship God are (i) to win lost people and (ii) to help God's people. At times "only a few things are necessary, really only one" (Luke 10:42), the simple worship of God! Yet we have chosen for the sake of simplicity and development to keep the next two purposes distinct from the first.

---

[1] *"Reprinted by permission. Rediscovering Pastoral Ministry: Shaping Contemporary Ministry with Biblical Mandates, by John MacArthur and Master's College Faculty, 1995, published Thomas Nelson Inc. Nashville, Tennessee. All rights reserved."*

13

**The second grand purpose of the church is to evangelise a lost world.** The church is to be a community witnessing to the saving grace of Christ. The Gospels are unanimous regarding the Great Commission given to the church by Christ (Matt. 28:18–20; Mark 16:15–16; Luke 24:46–47; John 17:18). The book of Acts not only concurs with this commission (1:8) but records the church's obedience to the Great Commission, from Jerusalem to the remotest part of the earth.

According to Ellen White, "Christ's last words to His disciples were: "Lo, I am with you always, even unto the end of the world." "Go ye therefore, and teach all nations." To us also the commission is given. We are bidden to go forth as Christ's messengers, to teach, instruct, and persuade men and women, to urge upon their attention the word of life. Go to the farthest bounds of the habitable globe, and know that wherever you go Christ's presence will attend you. (Ellen G White, Evangelism, 15)

MacArthur also mentions that **evangelism is not an option to be accepted or rejected by the church.** Outreach is a command. Evangelism is not limited to the gifted or to the church leadership. It is the mission of the entire church. To the truly faithful, evangelism is not merely a command but a compulsion (Acts 5:42; Rom. 1:14–17; 1 Cor. 9:16–18). Evangelism is the heart and soul of the New Testament church. (MacArthur)

The mandate is clear "that repentance for forgiveness of sins should be proclaimed in His name to all the nations, beginning from Jerusalem" (Luke 24:47–48). We are now living in the closing scenes of this world's history, said White. Let men and women tremble with the sense of the responsibility of knowing the truth. The ends of the world are come. In fact, "proper consideration of these things will lead all to make an entire consecration of all that they have and are to their God." (White, 15).

The obligation of warning a world of its coming doom is upon us. From every direction, far and near, calls are coming to us for help. The church, devotedly consecrated to the work, is to carry the message to the world: Come to the gospel feast; the supper is prepared, come. . . . Crowns, immortal crowns, are to be won. The kingdom of heaven is to be gained. A world, perishing in sin, is to be enlightened. The lost pearl is to be found. The lost sheep is to be brought back in safety to the fold. Who will join in the search? Who will bear the light to those who are wandering in the darkness.of error? (Ellen White, Review and Herald, July 23, 1895).

**Carrying out this purpose follows two approaches in Acts.** The first is contact with the lost in the immediate surroundings, whether it be the person next to us (Acts 2), the house next door (Acts 5:42), the next town (Acts 8:5), or people of a different ethnic makeup (Acts 10). The early church did not understand the Great Commission as a mandate to do speciality evangelism. There was but one church composed of all peoples (see Rev. 7:9).

**The second approach was to reach out to those in the regions beyond** (cf. Rom. 15:18–29), which involved commissioning special men with the mission of taking the gospel to the remotest parts of the earth (Acts 13:1–3). The church was not negligent in obeying the Lord's command, either in soul winning or in planting churches in other communities.

**The purpose of the church has not changed today.** The Great Commission still stands. Modern technology has not annulled it. Pressing social needs have not abrogated it. Spiritual problems in the church have not surpassed its importance. Neither Christ nor Paul would stay longer than necessary in one particular place. They moved on so that others might hear the gospel.

**In our biblical approach** to pastoral ministry, the pastor and church leadership (Conference presidents, secretariats, elders, treasurers, deacons, youth leaders, and all officers, must see their role in leading the congregation in fulfilling the Great Commission. The minister and ministry leaders is by Christ's design missionaries. Their church is to be a missionary church to those across the street or around the world. They are to be a world-class leader. They must have a vision beyond the pews in their facility. They should lead the way in praying for new fields, praying for God to thrust out labourers (Matt. 9:37–38), praying over the selection of missionaries (Acts 13:1–3), and supporting missionaries and the evangelistic enterprise. If they have a faithful minister, he can do no less and he dares not do otherwise.

# A Working Community

**The third purpose of the church** is to build itself up through the inter working of various members of the Body of Christ. The function of the Christian is to edify or spiritually build up fellow members in the Body of Christ. Getz states, "The church is to become a mature organization through the process of edification so that it will honour and glorify God."

The New Testament contains a number of references to this vital but neglected purpose of the church (Matt. 28:18–20; Acts 20:17–35; Rom. 12:1–8; 1 Cor. 12–14; Eph. 4:7–16; Col. 1:24–29; 1 Pet. 4:10–11). A summary of these texts is that God expects the church, which is a living organism, to grow spiritually in Christlikeness and that God has given every believer a unique spiritual gift that is intended not for self-growth but to enhance the spiritual development of fellow Christians. The role of the pastor, himself gifted for his task, is to help believers discover and utilize their gifts for the growth of the Body of Christ. A mature church can thus remain united, firm in its devotion to Christ, functioning according to the purpose of God, and able to stand against the attacks of Satan.

# Outreaching

**Why should evangelism be the concern of the church,** and why should involvement in evangelism be the ambition of the pastor?

**The answer is simple:** Our Lord Jesus told us to evangelise (Matt. 28:19–20; Mark 16:15–16; Luke 24:46–49; John 20:21; Acts 1:8). We are under obligation to fulfil the Great Commission to make disciples of all the nations, beginning with our own. The Lord's purpose, aim, and ambition is the salvation of mankind: "For even the Son of Man did not come to be served, but to serve, and to give His life a ransom for many" (Mark 10:45). "For the Son of Man has come to seek and to save that which was lost" (Luke 19:10). Winning the lost was for Christ the highest desire and was the express purpose for which He came into the world (John 4:32–33).

**Christ called the disciples to follow Him** and learn from Him to become "fishers of men" (Matt. 4:19). He schooled the disciples to become messengers of the kingdom news and witnesses of His sufferings. He ultimately commissioned them to evangelise the world, which they began doing as soon as they received power from the Holy Spirit (Acts 1:8; 2:1–4). The record in Acts describes the church's obedience to the Great Commission, the same commission entrusted to the church today.

# The Mandate for Outreaching

**The mandate, then, is to evangelise the world.** But what does evangelise mean? Some key definitions will clarify the meaning of evangelism. Packer defines evangelism as

*[ust preaching] the gospel, the evangel.... It is a work of communicating in which Christians make themselves mouthpieces for God's message of mercy to sinners. Anyone who faithfully delivers that message, under whatever circumstances, in a large meeting, in a small meeting, from a pulpit, or in private conversation, is EVANGELISING (J I Packer, Evangelism and the Sovereignty of God, 1961, 41).*

Any definition of evangelism or outreaching takes into consideration Matt. 28:18–20, which includes more than just a proclamation of a simple evangel. The command to "make disciples" includes at least four features:

**1. Going,** that is, taking the initiative to reach out to unreached people—we go to them, and do not expect them to come to us

**2. Presenting the gospel,** the message of the cross with all its implications of Christ's Lordship, atonement, grace, repentance, and faith

**3. Baptizing,** i.e., calling sinners into a public declaration of their faith in Christ and repentance from sin

**4. Teaching them;** forming converts into an assembly where the ongoing process of teaching is possible.

**Biblical outreaching** is more than dropping gospel leaflets over a city or inviting someone to a church concert. These four elements deserve a closer examination.

**1. Evangelism is proactive.** English translations of the original Greek text of Matt. 28:19 begin with "Go," which is the translation of an aorist participle conveying the sense "having gone." The main verb of the verse is "make disciples," or literally "disciple" all the nations. Hence, what the command assumes is that Christians will go out for the express purpose of making the nations disciples of Christ.

Biblical evangelism is outreaching, that is, going out to the lost souls of this world. Many have fallen into the error of thinking that if sinners among the nations want to be saved, they need to come to the church. The greatest single reason why the church is declining is that it has ceased to go out to the lost. For some reason, evangelism has become something to do in church—within the walls of the church building. The church today expects unbelievers to come to it, when in fact the church should go out to them. Effective outreach will take place when Christians realise that the starting point of the Great Commission is to move out from the comfort zones of ecclesiastical structures into the lives of the lost around them. From the pulpit to the pew—from the pastor to the parishioner—the perspective of evangelism must be that of a proactive, aggressive endeavour.

**2. Evangelism is gospel preaching.** The command to make disciples entails calling men and women to faith, obedience, and submission to Jesus Christ. Some equate evangelism with preaching social change, human rights, political liberation, economic equality, and many more causes. These issues, though they are righteous endeavours, are not biblical evangelism.

*The message*

Evangelism is the preaching of the cross of Christ, that He died for the sins of the world, that He arose from the dead, that He is Lord of the universe and of His church, and that people must believe the truth of the message before it can have any effect on their souls (Rom. 3:1–31; 10:9–10; 1 Cor. 15:1–4; Gal. 2;16–21). It must include the deity of Christ, His incarnation, His sinless nature, His vicarious substitutionary death for sinful humanity, His bodily resurrection, repentance and faith on the part of sinners, and the coming judgment of the world.

In recent times, it has been a tendency to water down the gospel of Christ. In an effort to make more converts, many have resorted to a diluted gospel void of the saving features. They have resorted to "another gospel," and inferior results are evident. An effective presentation of the true gospel will take careful preparation, time, thought, prayer, and patience. Evangelistic preaching is a call for souls to become disciples of Christ. Anything short of that is not biblical evangelism. Pleadings for professions of faith, decisions, or other outward manifestations just to elicit a response, if they do not result in making true disciples of the Lord Jesus, are not effective evangelism.

**3. Evangelism is transformed lives.** Christ commanded that the disciples baptize the nations into the triune name of God as a symbol of their turning from their sins to the Saviour. The gospel call is always "be saved from this perverse generation" (Acts 2:40) and "turn from these vain things to a living God" (Acts 14:15). The gospel is to let the nations know that God "is now declaring to men that all everywhere should repent" (Acts 17:30). It always involves "repentance toward God and faith in our Lord Jesus Christ" (Acts 20:21). Paul summed up his proclamation when he told King Agrippa that Christ called him to open the eyes of the Gentiles, "that they may turn from darkness to light, and from the domain of darkness to God, in order that they may receive forgiveness of sins and an inheritance among those who have been sanctified by faith in Me" (Acts 26:18). Hence effective biblical evangelism always results in changed lives, souls yielded to Christ, believers submitted to the Lordship of Christ.

**4. Evangelism is an ongoing discipleship.** The Lord included in the Great Commission the additional task of perfecting and maturing disciples by "teaching them to observe all that I commanded you" (Matt. 28:20). Effective evangelism has as its goal the incorporation of the disciple into the context of a local church or assembly of believers, where under the ministry and influence of gifted believers, the new disciple can grow into the fullness of the image of Christ (Eph. 4:11–16). New Testament evangelism issued from the local church and resulted in converts added to the local church. The measure of results was not the number of professions but the numbers added to the church, and later the number of churches formed through the churches' evangelistic outreach.

## The Manner of Outreaching

**With the mandates in mind,** the next step is to describe various ways of outreaching. The church in the New Testament used several methods for outreaching. Alex D. Montoya suggests that three of these main avenues are: (1) personal evangelism, (2) public evangelism, and (3) the planting of churches (MacArthur, Mayhue, and Thomas, part 4). In A brief glance at these three is sufficient:

### Personal Evangelism

The one to one approach to witnessing is still the best approach in outreaching. Each one reaching one with the word of Christ can make a tremendous difference in the church and life of a child of God. In fact, if we, the people of God, were actively involved in conversation with non-believers, there would be no need for public evangelism (evangelistic campaigns). Montoya suggests that "all evangelism is ultimately personal, with the heralder appealing to a lost soul either face-to-face or in a crowd." He said that "a person responds to the gospel in the privacy of his or her soul and in the uniqueness of the moment when the Holy Spirit lifts the veil, allowing that person to see the glory of the gospel. In that sense, all evangelism is personal" (MacArthur 306).

In the stricter sense, says Montoya, personal, one-2-one evangelism, is the effort of one person witnessing and leading another individual to Christ Jesus, so that He will become

EVANGELISING

their God and Saviour. It is an operation Andrew (where Andrew finds Simon Peter and witnessing to him about Christ- John 1:40–42). It is Philip finding Nathaniel (John 1:45). It is Jesus finding Nicodemus (John 3:1–5) and then the woman at the well (John 4:7–15). Therefore, personal evangelism was the first work of the disciples and the ministry that the Lord Jesus perfected superbly. It was the ongoing work of the early church, where daily from house to house they kept on preaching Jesus (Acts 5:42). The early witnesses to Christ, says Montoya, were renowned for their ability to engage in a personal wrestling to bring a soul to believe in Christ, as found in Acts 8:26–39; 20:20 (307).

**Public Evangelism**

Evangelism that is only targeting church members, is not public evangelism, but rather, revival. Acts chapter five provides us with the first public evangelism. In fact, Jesus, the disciples, and the early church made great use of public presentations of the gospel to large gatherings and crowds of all sorts. Peter's first two recorded evangelistic efforts (both public and a revival-reformation) at Pentecost and after, were to unusually large gatherings (of believers, but not believers in Christ Jesus as the Messiah and thus Saviour), yielded bountiful results—3,000 and 5,000 souls, respectively (Acts 2:14–41; 3:12–4:4). In acts 5:42, it can be seen that the disciples purposely sought a crowd that they might proclaim the cross of Christ more efficiently (ibid).

The early preachers designed their sermons not just to instruct believers but also to convert unbelievers. Some preaching today are at times deficient in addressing publicly the needs of the unconverted. The laity (those who want to mount the pulpit) must be trained in the public presentation (preaching) of the gospel to the lost and then make liberal use of such training in the numerous opportunities to preach evangelistically.

Montoya agrees with Ellen White, when he wrote saying

> Mass evangelism is not just for the mass evangelist. Every preacher of the Word must be ready to use public proclamation to do the work of an evangelist (2 Tim. 4:5). In every public forum exists a splendid opportunity to do public evangelism. Every generation has a certain group of unconverted people who frequent the halls of churches and will remain dead unless the preacher quickens them with the gospel. Dare to preach the gospel in church services for the sake of those who may need it.

**Planting Churches**

Within the last seven years, the idea of planting churches has resurfaced and we have seen a tremendous growth both here in the United Kingdom, as well as in USA. However, there must be some context to that which is now taking place, not so much as church planters 'x-change,' but rather, church planting as the end results of outreaching in the community.

**Biblically, as soon as the early disciples** reached out to their Jerusalem, Judea, and Samaria, they appears that they set about the task of reaching the remotest parts of the earth and EVANGELISING all the nations. These converts great distances away were obviously not going to belong to the church in Jerusalem. The only logical step was to plant churches in every city where they lived alongside lost men and women. Church planting was not a special pet project or an experimental endeavour; it was in direct fulfilment of the Great Commission. The apostles and disciples literally scattered themselves throughout the then-known world, EVANGELISING and planting churches in their wake (Aubrey Malphurs, Planting Growing Churches, 25).

**The church today fails** to see the correlation between evangelism and church planting, but any casual reading of the New Testament will quickly reverse this failure. Church planting is evangelism. Though not in agreement with all the

theological premises of Peter Wagner, I agree with this statement of his: "The single most effective evangelistic methodology under heaven is planting new churches.... Not to make an
explicit connection between evangelism and the local church is
a strategic blunder." Church planting is evangelism. If we care
about EVANGELISING communities, cities, and nations, we will
be aggressively planting new churches. A church planting ex-
pert states, "The idea is that planted churches reproduce themselves and make disciples by planting other churches. This is
a process that will continue until the Saviour returns. In fact,
this is the true meaning behind the Great Commission." Hence,
Great Commission churches are church-planting churches (C.
Peter Wagner, 11-12).

## Motivations of Outreaching

In Manuscript number 8, Ellen White wrote that "Christ has
given to every man his work, and we are to acknowledge the
wisdom of the plan He has made for us by a hearty cooperation with Him. It is in a life of service only that true happiness
is found. He who lives a useless, selfish life is miserable. He is
dissatisfied with himself and with everyone else" (White, 8MR
422).

She further adds that "true, unselfish, consecrated workers
gladly use their highest gifts in the lowliest service. They realize that true service means to see and to perform the duties
that God points out" (White, 8MR).

It is becoming more noticeable that **the vast majority of
Christians** in the United Kingdom and USA, do not evangelise,
and during the course of their lives will not lead one soul to
the Master. Some do not evangelise because they are ignorant
of the mechanics and substance of evangelism. Most, however,
do not evangelise because they lack the adequate motivation to
reach out to the lost or they live very busy lives with very little
time for personal evangelism.

Montoya believes that all believers should make every effort to place themselves on the highest plane in obedience to Christ. That one major area is that of motivating the shepherd. Where the shepherd is motivated, it will serves as a catalyst to prompt his people into a life of witnessing for the Saviour (310). Montoya suggests the following particular motivations for being actively engaged in evangelism.

**1. Obedience to Christ.** As undershepherd, pastors are under appointment from the Chief Shepherd, and it is their duty to evangelise the lost. They are not only responsible to feed the flock, they are to add to the flock by doing the work of an evangelist as well. The apostle Paul's great motive for preaching the gospel to the lost was his duty of fulfilling the stewardship given to him by Christ (1 Cor. 9:16–17). Green, in his masterful book Evangelism in the Early Church, states that from the beginning obedience to Christ was a major motivational factor for fulfilling the Great Commission. Early Christians felt it was "their responsibility before God to live lives consistent with their profession. The note of personal responsibility and accountability before God, the sovereign Judge, was a prominent spur to evangelism in the early church." Evangelism for the pastor is not a gift, nor is it an option. It is a command; one he should be careful to obey!

**2. Love of Christ.** Paul sets down the love of Christ as a motive for his ministry when he states, "For the love of Christ controls us" (2 Cor. 5:14). In the verses following, Paul gives several reasons for his persevering ministry of evangelising. Christ loves us, and He loves the world for which He died and thus wants the world redeemed and reconciled to Himself.

Love for Christ will motivate us to reach out to people, just as it motivated the early church. If we dearly love Christ and if we know anything of the love of Christ, we will be about the supreme task of sharing the love of Christ with others. How can we—how dare we do less?

**3. Love for mankind.** A genuine love for lost sinners also prompts evangelism. Enlightened souls with uplifted veils, who have experienced regeneration, escaped eternal torment, and received the pledge of the Holy Spirit, will naturally consider the dreadful plight of their fellow citizens. Compassion for the lost will move the hearts of Christians to reach out with the same remedy that quickened their own souls. The great apostle loved his own countrymen with affection so profound that it stoked the fires of his soul to agonize for their salvation. Paul twice testifies of his great love in his epistle to the Romans: "I have great sorrow and unceasing grief in my heart. For I could wish that I myself were accursed, separated from Christ for the sake of my brethren, my kinsmen according to the flesh" (Rom. 9:2–3). "Brethren, my heart's desire and my prayer to God for them is for their salvation" (Rom. 10:1). What love! What zeal!

**4. Outreaching has roots in love for sinners.** Love prompted God (John 3:16), love prompted Christ (Luke 19:10), and love prompted the early church.

It is a great contradiction to be called a child of God—even worse a Christian minister—without having love for lost souls. Packer says, "The wish to win the lost for Christ, should be ... The natural, spontaneous outflow of love in the heart of everyone who has been born again.

## Motivations for the People

White suggests one area where, because of possible belittling, the motivation necessary in encouraging our young people to become actively involved has deteriorated. She wrote,

> There must be no belittling of the gospel ministry. No enterprise should be so conducted as to cause the min-

istry of the word to be looked upon as an inferior matter. It is not so. Those who belittle the ministry are belittling Christ. The highest of all work is ministry in its various lines, and it should be kept before the youth that there is no work more blessed of God than that of the gospel minister (6T 411).

Therefore, next to motivating the pastor for outreaching, the second greatest need is to motivate rank-and-file Christians to be about this vital work of soul winning (Montoya, 310). The average Christian needs to be on fire with a white-hot zeal for lost souls. "How enormous and wonderful and glorious would be the result," writes Torrey, "if all Christians should begin to be active personal workers to the extent of their ability!" In fact, the greatest moments of outreaching in church history have come through efforts by the masses of average believers (R. A. Torrey 11).

Church historian Latourette states, "The chief agents in the expansion of Christianity appear not to have been those who made it a profession or made it a major part of their occupation, but men and women who carried on their livelihood in some purely secular manner and spoke of their faith to those they met in this natural fashion" (K. S. Latourette 116–17).

According to Ellen White

That which is needed now for the upbuilding of our churches is the nice work of wise labourers to discern and develop talent in the church, talent that can be educated for the Master's use. There should be a well organized plan for the employment of workers to go into all our churches, large and small, to instruct the members how to labour for the upbuilding of the church, and also for unbelievers. It is training, education, that is needed. Those who labour in visiting the churches should give the brethren and sisters instruction in practical methods of doing missionary work. (White, Testimonies, vol. 9 117)

Church leaders need to mobilise, motivate, equip, and unleash their churches on the unchurched communities where they stand. Evangelism never was nor can it be the work of only the professional, the pastor, or a select few. It is the prerogative and privilege of the masses in our churches. They need equipping and motivation to do the job (Montoya 311). Said White, "there should be no delay in this well-planned effort to educate the church members"(119).

**Some believers do not evangelise** because they have never received instruction in how to evangelise. Others do not evangelise because they have never seen the need to evangelise. Still others do not carry on an active part in evangelism because they do not have new opportunities to share their faith. Every pastor should urge evangelistic activity upon his parishioners, train them for it, and see that they do it.

What can the pastor do to motivate his people? Consider five suggestions, by Montoya, for accomplishing this:

**1. The pastor motivates by his example.** The Lord said to His disciples, "Follow Me, and I will make you fishers of men" (Matt. 4:19).

**2. The pastor motivates by his expectations.** Most behaviour is learned behaviour. Hence, in evangelism people will eventually do what is expected of them.

**3. The pastor motivates by his exhortations.** The pastor as the chief speaker is also the best motivator, and he ought to make use of his charisma in the pulpit to excite the people into soul winning. Sermons on personal evangelism ought to heat up the yearly preaching schedule.

**4. The pastor motivates with the excitement of new converts.** The best way to prime the pump of evangelism is by means of new believers being added to the church.

**5. The pastor motivates by promoting special evangelistic efforts.** Even in the finest of circumstances, churches can reach a point where the number of lost people accessible to the church dwindles dramatically. Special efforts are necessary to provide Christians with new opportunities to share their faith. These can be in the form of evangelistic rallies held in the church or sites conducive to evangelism, citywide crusades, evangelistic home Bible studies, literature distribution campaigns, short-term missionary trips, evangelistic sport programs, and the like. The point here is that these events do not just happen. They need planning and promotion, and usually that begins with the pastor or the church leaders. Here is an excellent and exciting way to get a large portion of the church involved in evangelism, but the key again is the pastor. These events need his support and aggressive endorsement.

# Methods for Outreaching

According to Ellen White,

> Christ ministered to people's needs before inviting them to follow Him. Christ's method alone will give true success in reaching the people. The Saviour mingled with men as one who desired their good. He showed His sympathy for them, ministered to their needs, and won their confidence. Then He bade them, "Follow Me (White, Pastoral Ministry, 117.)

Following Christ method, said White, would empower us and enable us to fulfil the mission and ministry given to the church. She suggests that we should:

*P*
*L*
*A*
*N*

**1. Devise methods to reach the people where they are.** That we should let every worker in the Master's vineyard, study, plan, devise methods, to reach the people where they are. Furthermore, we must do something out of the common course of things. We must arrest the attention. We must be deadly in earnest. This is because we are on the very verge of times of trouble and perplexities that are scarcely dreamed of. (White, Evangelism, 122, 123.)

*S*
*H*
*A*
*R*
*E*

**2. Become like a "beehive" church.** A beehive church will have a multifaceted programme for reaching the community (strategic plans for reaching the churches community. Strategic because it is to be a deliberate, definite plan and not haphazard.) White demonstrates what she meant by using the "beehive" in San Francisco. She said

> During the past few years the "beehive" in San Francisco has been indeed a busy one. Many lines of Christian effort have been carried forward by our brethren and sisters there. These included visiting the sick and destitute, finding homes for orphans and work for the unemployed, nursing the sick, and teaching the truth from house to house, distributing literature, and conducting classes on healthful living and the care of the sick. A school for the children has been conducted in the basement of the Laguna Street meetinghouse. For a time a workingmen's home and medical mission was maintained. On Market Street, near the city hall, there were treatment rooms, operated as a branch of the St. Helena Sanitarium. In the same locality was a health-food store. Nearer the centre of the city, not far from the Call building, was conducted a vegetarian cafe, which was open six days in the week and entirely closed on the Sabbath. Along the water front, ship mission work was carried on. At various times our ministers conducted meetings in large halls in the city. Thus the warning message was given by many (White, Pastoral Ministry, 117.)

The Seeker for soul must not give up, even though the going is difficult. The worker may find it complicated, but lessons learnt from the three lost things in the gospel of Luke chapter 19, should encourage the worker to continue his/her outreach activities. Accordingly, White wrote

> Seek until you have the joy of finding. The lesson of persevering faith and labour Christ Himself has taught us. In the parable of the lost sheep He has presented to our imagination no picture of a sorrowful shepherd returning without the sheep. The shepherd's search ceases not until the lost is brought back to the fold. The woman whose coin is lost searches till she finds it. These parables do not speak of failure but of success and joy in the recovery of the lost. Here is the divine guarantee that not one lost soul is overlooked, not one is left unsuccored. With all our efforts in seeking for the lost, Christ will cooperate (White, Pastoral Ministry, 117)

In contrast, White wrote, as a warning, that

> Those who gather the sunshine of Christ's righteousness, and do not let it shine forth into the lives of others, will soon lose the sweet, bright rays of heavenly grace, selfishly reserved to be lavished only upon a few. Those who possess much affection are responsible to God to bestow this affection . . . on all who need help. . . . (White, OHC 231.)

**In the next section**, some key encouragements/motivational materials from Ellen G White will be provided in seeking to clear up any misunderstandings regarding Public campaigns. In addition, I will provide some materials (from my resource) that might be useful in developing a better   approach to such meetings.

# PLANNING THE CAMPAIGN

Excerpts from Ellen G. White, Evangelism

*Strategic planning: The way to identify and move toward desired future states. It is the process of developing and implementing plans to reach goals and objectives.*

*In this section, I have reproduced some of the guidelines given by Ellen White, because they are extremely valuable to those planning evangelistic meetings.*

# 3

## PLANNING THE CAMPAIGN
Reproduced from Ellen G White, Evangelism

The planning of a local church evangelistic campaign must start with prayer and prayer must continue throughout the whole campaign.

There should be a programme of prayer in a number of different ways. It should include house prayer meetings, church prayer groups, and individual quiet time prayer for the evangelistic campaign (revival). After the praying for the planning has begun, the planning can begin.

Planning will require the use of several committees. Committees similar to those used for Charles D. Brookes, Walter Pearson, Mark Finley, and other mass evangelistic campaigns can also be used for church evangelism. Committees needed are prayer, publicity, counselling, ushers, outreach, youth, music, and soul-winning committees (see chapter on Job description for a comprehensive list of committees needed).

The promoting of an evangelistic campaign will require extensive use of the media. The publicity committee will use the newspapers, television, radio, and even tracts in stores or passed out at the local super stores.

A committee to call all church members, active and inactive to support the campaign with their presence is a good idea. The pastor or campaign coordinator has to promote the campaign everywhere. Soul-winning training should be conducted and visits made prior to the campaign. Proper planning, promoting, and prayer are the keys to a good evangelistic campaign.

According to Ellen White, there are several areas that the team should consider during the planning of the campaign:

1. Understanding Christ's Method and Approach
2. Planning an Aggressive Work
3. Planning Ahead for new churches/New Openings
4. Planning the Campaign Programme
5. Looking at the Evangelist and His Team
6. How to Hold Large audiences
7. Incorporating Spiritually Gifted Teachers
8. Plan for the Work
9. The Evangelistic Site for the campaign
10. Financing the campaign

**Study Christ's Methods**. If ever it has been essential that we understand and follow right methods of teaching and follow the example of Christ, it is now. (White,  Ev 53)

## Meeting People

**How He Met the People**. If you would approach the people acceptably, humble your hearts before God, and learn His ways. We shall gain much instruction for our work from a study of Christ's methods of labour and His manner of meeting the people. In the gospel story we have the record of how He worked for all classes, and of how as He laboured in cities and towns, thousands were drawn to His side to hear His teaching. The words of the Master were clear and distinct, and were spoken in sympathy and tenderness. They carried with them the assurance that here was truth. It was the simplicity and earnestness with which Christ laboured and spoke that drew so many to Him (White, Ev 53).

The great Teacher laid plans for His work. Study these plans. We find Him travelling from place to place, followed by crowds of eager listeners. When He could, He would lead them away from the crowded cities, to the quiet of the country. Here he would pray with them, and talk to them of eternal truths (White, Ev 53).

## Christ's Method of Outreach

**Methods Peculiarly His Own**. He attended the great yearly festivals of the nation, and to the multitude absorbed in outward ceremony He spoke of heavenly things, bringing eternity within their view. To all He brought treasures from the storehouse of wisdom. He spoke to them in language so simple that they could not fail of understanding. By methods peculiarly His own, He helped all who were in sorrow and affliction. With tender, courteous grace, He ministered to the sin-sick soul, bringing healing and strength. (White, Ev 54).

**The Prince of teachers**:

1. **He sought access to the people** by the pathway of their most familiar associations.
2. **He presented the truth** in such a way that ever after it was to His hearers intertwined with their most hallowed recollections and sympathies.

3. **He taught in a way** that made them feel the completeness of His identification with their interests and happiness.

4. **His instruction was so direct**, His illustrations were so appropriate, His words so sympathetic and cheerful, that His hearers were charmed. The simplicity and earnestness with which He addressed the needy, hallowed every word (White, Ministry of Healing, 22-24).

PLANNING CAMPAIGN

5. **Jesus Studied Faces**-Even the crowd that so often thronged His steps was not to Christ an indiscriminate mass of human beings. He spoke directly to every mind and appealed to every heart (White, Ev 55)

6. **He watched the faces of His hearers,** marked the lighting up of the countenance, the quick, responsive glance, which told that truth had reached the soul; and there vibrated in His heart the answering chord of sympathetic joy (White, Education, 231).

7. **Appeal of Fallen Humanity**. In every human being, however fallen, He beheld a son of God, one who might be restored to the privilege of His divine relationship (White, Education, 79).

8. **Simplicity, Directness, Repetition.** Christ's teaching was simplicity itself. He taught as one having authority. He proclaimed the truth to humanity, many of whom could not be educated in the schools of the rabbis, neither in Greek philosophy. Jesus uttered truth in a plain, direct manner, giving vital force and impressiveness to all His utterances. Had He raised His voice to an unnatural key, as is customary with many preachers in this day, the pathos and melody of the human voice would have been lost, and much of the force of the truth destroyed. (Ev 55).

9. **In His discourses** Christ did not bring many things before them at once, lest He might confuse their minds. He made every point clear and distinct. He did not disdain the repetition of old and familiar truths in prophecies if they would serve His purpose to inculcate ideas (Ev 56).

10. **He Charmed the Greatest Minds**. Although the great truths uttered by our Lord were given in simple language, they were clothed with such beauty that they interested and charmed the greatest intellects. (White, Ev 56)

11. **He Reset Gems in the Framework of Truth.** In His teachings Christ did not sermonize as ministers do today. His work was to build upon the framework of truth. He gathered up the precious gems of truth which had been appropriated by the enemy and placed in the framework of error, and reset them in the framework of truth, that all who received the word might be enriched thereby (White, Manuscript 104, 1898; Ev 57).

12. **He Reinforced the Message**. Christ was always ready to answer the sincere inquirer after truth. When His disciples came to Him for an explanation of some word He had spoken to the multitude, He gladly repeated His lesson (White, Letter 164, 1902; Ev 57)

13. **He Drew by Love**. Christ drew the hearts of His hearers to Him by the manifestation of His love, and then, little by little, as they were able to bear it, He unfolded to them the great truths of the kingdom. We also must learn to adapt our labours to the condition of the people to meet men where they are. While the claims of the law of God are to be presented to the world, we should never forget that love, the love of Christ, is the only power that can soften the heart and lead to obedience (Review and Herald, Nov. 25, 1890; Ev 57).

14. **He Restrained Truth**. The great Teacher held in His hand the entire map of truth, but He did not disclose it all to His disciples. He opened to them those subjects only which were essential to their advancement in the path of heaven. There were many things in regard to which His wisdom kept Him silent (Ev 57).

As Christ withheld many things from His disciples, knowing that then it would be impossible for them to comprehend; so today He withholds many things from us, knowing the limited capacity of our understanding (Manuscript 118, 1902. 58.)

PLANNING CAMPAIGN

### Christ's Approach

**In Personal Interviews**. The work of Christ was largely composed of personal interviews. He had a faithful regard for the one-soul audience; and that one soul has carried to thousands the intelligence received (Review and Herald, May 9, 1899; Ev 58).

**At the Feasts**. When invited to a feast, Christ accepted the invitation, that He might, while sitting at the table, sow the seeds of truth in the hearts of those present. He knew that the seed thus sown would spring up and bring forth fruit. He knew that some of those sitting at meat with Him would afterward respond to His call, "Follow Me." Ours is the privilege of studying Christ's manner of teaching as He went from place to place, everywhere sowing the seeds of truth (Manuscript 113, 1902; Ev 58).

**Christ's Follow-up Plan** (Preparation for the campaign). Christ sent out His disciples two and two, to go to places to which He would afterward follow (Manuscript 19, 1910; Ev 58)

The Majesty of heaven journeyed from place to place on foot, teaching out of doors by the seaside, and in the mountain. Thus He drew the people to Him. Are we greater than our Lord? Was His way the right way? Have we been working unwisely in maintaining simplicity and godliness? We have not learned our lesson yet as we should. Christ declares, Take My yoke of restraint and obedience upon you, and ye shall find rest unto your souls. For My yoke is easy, and My burden is light (Letter 140, 1898; Ev 58).

# Planning An Expanding Evangelism
(White, Evangelism, 59-60)

**The Time for an Aggressive Work**. To all people and nations and kindred and tongues the truth is to be proclaimed. The time has come for much aggressive work to be done in the cities, and in all neglected, unworked fields (Review and Herald, June 23, 1904; Ev 59).

**Wise Plans.** Diligent work is now called for. In this crisis, no halfhearted efforts will prove successful. In all our city work, we are to hunt for souls. Wise plans are to be laid, in order that such work may be done to the best possible advantage (Review and Herald, Sept. 27, 1906; Ev 59).

**Launching Out Into the Deep**. There are those who think it is their duty to preach the truth, but they dare not venture from the shore, and they catch no fish. They will choose to go among the churches, over and over the same ground. They report a good time, a pleasant visit, but we look in vain for the souls that are converted to the truth through their instrumentality. These ministers hug the shore too closely. Let them launch out into the deep, and cast their net where the fish are. There is no lack of work to be done. There could be hundreds employed in the vineyard of the Lord where there is now one (The True Missionary, February, 1874; Ev 59).

**A Challenge to the Leaders.** I ask those who have charge of our work: Why are so many places passed by? Look upon the towns and cities yet unworked. There are many large cities in America, not only in the South, but in the North, yet to be worked. In every city in America there should be some memorial for God. But I could mention many places where the light of truth has not yet shone. The angels of heaven are waiting for human instrumentalities to enter the places where witness has not yet been borne to present truth (White, Ev 60).

PLANNING CAMPAIGN

**Clear New Ground-Establish New Centres.** Prepare workers to go out in the highways and hedges. We need wise nurserymen who will transplant trees to different localities and give them advantages, that they may grow. It is the positive duty of God's people to go into the regions beyond. Let forces be set at work to clear new ground, to establish new centres of influence wherever an opening can be found (Manuscript 11, 1908; Ev 60).

**Reach Beyond the Gospel-hardened Centres.** Let us remember that as a people entrusted with sacred truth, we have been neglectful and positively unfaithful. The work has been confined to a few centres, until the people in them have become gospel hardened. It is difficult to make an impression on those who have heard so much truth and yet have rejected it. In a few places too much has been expended, while many, cities have been left unwarned and unworked (Ev 60).

# Planning Ahead for New Openings.
(White, Evangelism, 62-63)

Oh, how I seem to hear the voice day and night, "Go forward; add new territory; enter new territory with the tent, and give the last message of warning to the world. There is no time to be lost. Leave My memorial in every place where ye shall go. My Spirit will go before you, and the glory of the Lord shall be your rearward" (White, Ev 62).

There are other towns not a long distance from here, which must have a camp meeting (camp meetings proceeded campaigns) next year. This is the very plan of God how the work should be carried. Those who have had the light for years to enter new fields with the tent, and have held the camp meetings in the same ground for years, need to be converted themselves, because they do not heed the word of the Lord (White, Letter 174, 1900; Ev 61).

**1. Advance in Faith**-Means Will Come. Can we expect the inhabitants of these cities to come to us and say, "If you will come to us and preach, we will help you to do thus and so"? They know nothing of our message. The Lord desires us to let our light so shine before men that His Holy Spirit may communicate the truth to the honest in heart who are seeking after truth. As we do this work, we shall find that means will flow into our treasuries, and we shall have means with which to carry on a still broader and more far-reaching work (Ev 61).

**2. Follow God's Opening Providence.** If we would follow the opening providence of God, we should be quick to discern every opening, and make the most of every advantage within our reach. . . . There is a fearfulness to venture out and run risks in this great work, fearing that the expenditure of means would not bring returns. What if means are used and yet we cannot see that souls have been saved by it? What if there is a dead loss of a portion of our means? Better work and keep at work than to do nothing. You know not which shall prosper-this or that (Ev 62).

Men will invest in patent rights and meet with heavy losses, and it is taken as a matter of course. But in the work and cause of God, men are afraid to venture. Money seems to them to be a dead loss that does not bring immediate returns when invested in the work of saving souls. The very means that is now so sparingly invested in the cause of God, and that is selfishly retained, will in a little while be cast with all idols to the moles and to the bats. Money will soon depreciate in value very suddenly when the reality of eternal scenes opens to the senses of man (Ev 62).

God will have men who will venture anything and everything to save souls. Those who will not move until they can see every step of the way clearly before them will not be of advantage at this time to forward the truth of God. There must be workers now who will push ahead in the dark as well as in

PLANNING CAMPAIGN

the light, and who will hold up bravely under discouragements and disappointed hopes, and yet work on with faith, with tears and patient hope, sowing beside all waters, trusting the Lord to bring the increase. God calls for men of nerve, of hope, faith, and endurance, to work to the point. (The True Missionary, January, 1874; Ev 63).

**3. Be Resourceful.** In these perilous times we should leave untried no means of warning the people. We should be deeply interested in everything that will stay the tide of iniquity. Work on. Have faith in God. (Letter 49, 1902; Ev 63).

**4. Not in Our Own Strength.** I appeal to you, my brethren in the ministry. Connect yourselves more closely with the work of God. Many souls that might be saved, will be lost, unless you strive more earnestly to make your work as perfect as possible. There is a great work to be done in-----. It may seem to move slowly and hard at first; but God will work mightily through you if you will only make an entire surrender to Him. Much of the time you will have to walk by faith, not by feeling. . . . (Ev 63).

Wherever you are, however trying your circumstances, do not talk discouragement. The Bible is full of rich promises. Can you not believe them? When we go out to labour for souls, God does not want us to go a warfare at our own charges. What does this mean? It means that we need not go in our own strength, for God has pledged His word that He will go with us (Historical Sketches, 128, 129).

**5. Leave Results With God.** The good seed sown may lie some time in a cold, worldly, selfish heart, without evidencing that it has taken root; but frequently the Spirit of God operates upon that heart, and waters it with the dew of heaven, and the long-hidden seed springs up and finally bears fruit to the glory of God. We know not in our lifework which shall prosper, this or that. These are not questions for us poor mortals to settle. We are to do our work, leaving the result with God (Testimonies, vol. 3, p. 248; Ev 64).

PLANNING CAMPAIGN

# Planning The Campaign Programme[1]

It is suggested that, where the venue is a Marquee, the evangelistic team should endeavour to incorporate several activities that may attract people to the venue and thereby to the meetings. In previous years, we have all seen the facilities, with security, but with nothing taking place. In contrast, it is possible to have other activities taking place at the Marquee, outside of the planned campaign programme. These programmes should take on a holistic approach; for example, I would recommend that there is something for everyone i.e. in the family; mother, father, children and grandparents.

It is also a good idea to try and schedule the campaign to run into one of the children's school holidays, i.e. half term, Easter holiday etc.

By so doing, it is possible to focus one subsidiary presentation on a current community issue/problem area.

It is very important that what is presented is carefully crafted to begin and end as a total package (Parenting package, teens package, Health package, toddlers package, non smoking package etc.) In addition, it is possible that we could also include a period of praying and anointing of those in poor health, throughout the day or alternatively, a drop-in prayer session for the local area.

### A typical day could be:

| | |
|---|---|
| 09.00 - 09.45 | A review/ feedback (pastor, team leaders/ coordinators) |
| 10.00 - 11.30 | Specialist in/outside member/team/agency could talk to local parents about coping and managing children's behaviour |
| 12.00 - 13.00 | Lunch Time prayer Meeting (Prayer Ministry Department) |

---

1 *Esther Fleary-Griffiths, Planning the Campaign Programme, February 2009, np.*

| | |
|---|---|
| 14.00 - 15.00 | Cooking and Eating Healthy- Cookery demonstration and a short talk from a Dietician (Health Ministry) |
| 16.00 -17.30 | Children's hour (story, art activity, prayer by Children's Ministry) |
| 18.00 - 19.00 | Creating a work Life Balance presentation (Family Life) |
| 19.30 - 21.00 | Campaign series |
| 21.00 - 21.30 | Team Prayer/ feedback session |

# The Evangelist and His Team
(White, Evangelism, 69-72)

**Evangelism and Evangelists.** When I think of the cities in which so little work has been done, in which there are so many thousands to be warned of the soon coming of the Saviour, I feel an intensity of desire to see men and women going forth to the work in the power of the Spirit filled with Christ's love for perishing souls.

My mind is deeply stirred. In every city there is work to be done. Labourers are to go into our large cities and hold camp meetings. In these meetings, the very best talent is to be employed, that the truth may be proclaimed with power. Men of varied gifts are to be brought in.

**New methods must be introduced.** God's people must awake to the necessities of the time in which they are living. God has men whom He will call into His service, men who will not carry forward the work in the lifeless way in which it has been carried forward in the past.

**In our large cities** the message is to go forth as a lamp that burned. God will raise up Labourers for this work, and His angels will go before them. Let no one hinder these men of God's

44

appointment. Forbid them not. God has given them their work. Let the message be given with so much power that the hearers shall be convinced.

**Strong Men Needed**. I call upon our ministering brethren to consider this matter. Let strong men be appointed to work in the great centres.

**A Variety of Talent**. In our tent meetings we must have speakers who can make a good impression on the people. The ability of one man, however intelligent this man may be, is insufficient to meet the need. A variety of talents should be brought into these meetings.

**Second Man a Good Investment (paid workers)**. The Lord designs that His work shall be carried solidly. To enter a new field involves large expense. But the extra expense of a second man to help will be an investment that will bring returns. I feel to urge this matter because so much is at stake. I pray the Lord to impress your minds to carry out His will.

# Holding Large Audiences.
(White, Evangelism, 69-72)

The Lord has given to some ministers the ability to gather and to hold large congregations. As they labour in the fear of God, the deep moving of the Holy Spirit upon human hearts. Will attend their efforts.

**I am charged to wake up the watchmen**. The end of all things is at hand. Now is the accepted time. Let our ministers and presidents of conferences exercise their tact and skill in presenting the truth before large numbers of people in our cities. As you labour in simplicity, hearts will be melted. Bear in mind that as you deliver the testing message for this time, your own heart will be softened and quickened by the subdu-

PLANNING CAMPAIGN

45

ing influence of the Holy Spirit, and you will have souls for your hire. As you stand before multitudes in the cities, remember that God is your helper, and that by His blessing you may bear a message of a character to reach the hearts of the hearers.

## Incorporate Spiritually Gifted Teachers

**Men and Women to Teach Truth.** Wise teachers -men and women who are apt in teaching the truths of the Word- are needed in our cities. Let these present the truth in all its sacred dignity, and with sanctified simplicity.

**Paul a Travelling Evangelist.** Paul's was a life of intense and varied activities. From city to city, from country to country, he journeyed, telling the story of the cross, winning converts to the gospel, and establishing churches (Gospel Workers, 58, 59).

**Strong, Courageous Workers.** Feeble or aged men and women should not be sent to labour in unhealthful, crowded cities. Let them labour where their lives will not be needlessly sacrificed. Our brethren who bring the truth to the cities must not be obliged to imperil their health in the noise and bustle and confusion, if retired places can be secured (Ev 71).

Those who are engaged in the difficult and trying work in the cities should receive every encouragement possible. Let them not be subjected to unkind criticism from their brethren. We must have a care for the Lord's workers who are opening the light of truth to those who are in the darkness of error (Ev 72)

**Advantages of Two and Two.** Jesus Sent Out Brother With Brother. Calling the twelve about Him, Jesus bade them go out two and two through the towns and villages. None were sent forth alone, but brother was associated with brother, friend with friend. Thus they could help and encourage each other, counselling and praying together, each one's strength supplementing the other's weakness. In the same manner He afterward sent forth the seventy.

It was the Saviour's purpose that the messengers of the gospel should be associated in this way. In our own time evangelistic work would be far more successful if this example were more closely followed (The Desire of Ages, 350).

# God's Plan for the Work Today
(White, Evangelism, 72-74)

**When Jesus sent His disciples forth to labour,** . . . They did not feel as some do now, that they would rather work alone than have anyone with them who did not labour just as they laboured. Our Saviour understood what ones to associate together. He did not connect with the mild, beloved John one of the same temperament; but He connected with him the ardent, impulsive Peter. These two men were not alike either in their disposition or in their manner of labour. Peter was prompt and zealous in action, bold and uncompromising, and would often wound; John was ever calm, and considerate of others' feelings, and would come after to bind up and encourage. Thus the defects in one were partially covered by the virtues in the other (Ev 72)

**God never designed that, as a rule,** His servants should go out singly to labour. To illustrate: Here are two brothers. They are not of the same temperament; their minds do not run in the same channel. One is in danger of doing too much; the other fails to carry the burdens that he should. If associated together, these might have a molding influence upon each other, so that the extremes in their characters would not stand out so prominently in their labours. It might not be necessary for them to be together in every meeting; but they could labour in places ten, fifteen or even thirty miles apart,

PLANNING CAMPAIGN

near enough together, however, so that if one came to a crisis in his labours, he could call on the other for assistance. They should also come together as often as possible for prayer and consultation. . . . (Ev 73)

When one labours alone continually, he is apt to think that his way is above criticism, and he feels no particular desire to have anyone labour with him. But it is Christ's plan that someone should stand right by his side, so that the work shall not be molded entirely by one man's mind, and so that his defects of character shall not be regarded as virtues by himself or by those who hear him. (Ev 73)

**Unless a speaker has one by his side** with whom he can share the labour, he will many times be placed in circumstances where he will be obliged to do violence to the laws of life and health. Then, again, important things sometimes transpire to call him away right in the crisis of an interest. If two are connected in labour, the work at such times need not be left alone. Historical Sketches, pp. 126, 127. (1886)

**Advantages of United Labour.** There is need of two working together; for one can encourage the other, and they can counsel, pray, and search the Bible together. In this they may get a broader light upon the truth; for one will see one phase, and the other another phase of the truth. If they are erring, they can correct one another in speech and attitude, so that the truth may not be lightly esteemed because of the defects of its advocates. If the workers are sent out alone, there is no one to see or correct their errors; but when two go together, an educating work may be carried on, and each worker become what he should be a successful soul winner (Ev 74.1).

# The Evangelistic Site
(White, Evangelism, 74-76)

**1. "Study Your Location."** Enter the large cities, and create an interest among the high and the low. Make it your work to preach the gospel to the poor, but do not stop there. Seek to reach the higher classes also. Study your location with a view to letting your light shine forth to others. This work should have been done long since (Testimonies to Ministers, 400; Ev 74).

**2. Work in Halls.** Let halls be hired, and let the message be given with such power that the hearers will be convinced. God will raise up workers who will occupy peculiar spheres of influence, workers who will carry the truth to the most unpromising places (Manuscript 127, 1901; Ev 75.1).

**3. Large Halls in Our Cities.** The large halls in our cities should be secured, that the third angel's message may be proclaimed by human lips. Thousands will appreciate the message (Letter 35, 1895; Ev 75).

**4. The Most Popular Halls.** It requires money to carry the message of warning to the cities. It is sometimes necessary to hire at large expense the most popular halls, in order that we may call the people out. Then we can give them Bible evidence of the truth (Manuscript 114, 1905; Ev 75.3).

**5. Begin Cautiously.** I have been and still am instructed regarding the necessities required for the work in the cities. We must quietly secure buildings, without defining all we intend to do. We must use great wisdom in what we say, lest our way be hedged up. Lucifer is an ingenious worker, drawing from our people all possible knowledge, that he may, if possible, defeat the plans laid to arouse our cities. On some points silence is eloquence (Letter 84, 1910; Ev 75).

**6. Lease Good Halls.** In some places the work must begin in a small way, and advance slowly. This is all that the Labour-

PLANNING CAMPAIGN

ers can do. But in many cases a wider and more decided effort might be made at the outset, with good results. The work in ___ Might now be much further advanced than it is if our brethren, at the beginning of the work there, had not tried to work in so cheap a way. If they had hired good halls, and carried forward the work as though we had great truths, which would surely be victorious, they would have had greater success. God would have the work started in such a way that the first impressions given shall be, as far as they go, the very best that can be made (Gospel Workers, 462; Ev 75).

**7. Tents Pitched in Most Favourable Places.** We must carry the truth to the cities. Tents are to be pitched in the most favourable places, and meetings held (Ev 76).

# Finance and the Budget
(White, Evangelism, 85-87)

**1. Sit Down and Count the Cost.** God's people are not to go forward blindly in the investment of means that they have not and know not where to obtain. We must show wisdom in the movements that we make. Christ has laid before us the plan upon which His work is to be conducted. Those who desire to build must first sit down and count the cost, to see whether they are able to carry the building to completion. Before they begin to carry out their plans, they must advise with wise counsellors. If one worker, failing to reason from cause to effect, is in danger of making unwise moves, his fellow workers are to speak words of wisdom to him, showing him where he is in error ( Letter 182, 1902;Ev 85)

**2. Strict Economy.** Let all who take up the work in our large cities be careful in this respect-in no place should there be any needless expenditure of money. It is not by outward display that men and women are to learn what is comprehended by present truth. Our workers are to practice strict economy. God forbids all extravagance. Every dollar at our command is to be expended with economy. No great display is to be made. God's money is to be used to carry forward in His own way the work that He has declared must be done in our world (Letter 107, 1905; Ev 85).

**3. Begin Without Display**. Why should we delay to begin work in our cities? We are not to wait for some wonderful things to be done, or some costly apparatus to be provided, in order that a great display may be made. What is the chaff to the wheat? If we walk and work humbly before God, He will prepare the way before us (Letter 335, 1904; Ev 86).

**4. Balanced Evangelism**. God forbid that there should be a large outlay of means in a few places, without considering the needs of the many fields that have scarcely any help. Self-denial exercised by the brethren in favoured localities in order that adequate help may be given to needy fields, will aid in accomplishing a work that will bring glory to God. None can afford to build a high tower of influence in one locality, while they leave other places unworked. The Lord grant that our senses may be sanctified, and that we may learn to measure our ideas by the work and the teachings of Christ (Letter 320, 1908; Ev 86).

**5. Bearing Expense of a Worker.** In the great cities many agencies are to be set at work. Those who are so situated that they cannot act a part in personal labour, may interest themselves in bearing the expenses of a labourer who can go. Let not our brethren and sisters make excuses for not engaging in earnest work. No practical Christian lives to himself (Manuscript 128, 1901; Ev 86).

**6. Churches Finance New Work.** Those who know the truth are to strengthen one another, saying to the ministers, "Go forth into the harvest field in the name of the Lord, and our prayers shall go with you as sharp sickles." Thus our churches should bear decided witness for God, and they should also bring Him their gifts and offerings, that those who go forth into the field may have wherewith to labour for soul (Manuscript 73a, 1900; Ev 86).

PLANNING CAMPAIGN

**7. God's Provision for City Work.** I have had messages from the Lord, which I have given to our people over and over again, that there are many monied men who are susceptible to the influences and impressions of the gospel message. The Lord has a people who have never yet heard the truth. Keep to your work, and let the property that shall be donated to the advancement of the truth be so used that a centre shall be established in ____. Let proper persons, who have never revealed the selfish, grasping spirit which withholds the means that ought to be used in the large cities, be selected to carry forward the work, because God acknowledges them as His chosen ones (Ev 87).

8. God will move upon the hearts of monied men, when the Bible, and the Bible alone, is presented as the light of the world. In these cities the truth is to go forth as a lamp that burneth (Ev 87).

# SAMPLE CAMPAIGN BUDGET
## Illustration No.1
A Four Week Evangelistic Campaign
Days: Saturday, Sunday, Tuesday, Wednesday, and Friday

## Proposed Income

| | |
|---|---|
| Church (voted at Business Meeting) | £ 4,500.00 |
| Offerings (guesstimate at £30 per night x 4 weeks) | £ 600.00 |
| Area Allocation (for church via Area) | £ 2 500.00 |
| Request to Area/District Advisory Council | £ 2,000.00 |
| Request to Conference (Personal Ministries Dept.) | £ 900.00 |
| Miscellaneous/Gifts | £ 200.00 |
| **Total Income** | **£10,700.00** |

## Proposed Expenditure

| | |
|---|---|
| Hire of Hall | £4,200.00 |
| Speaker (flight, travel, accommodation, and meals) | £2,600.00 |
| Bible Workers (transport and Stipend) | £ 900.00 |
| Bibles and Lesson booklets | £ 200.00 |
| P A Equipment Hire | £ 600.00 |
| Literature | £ 250.00 |
| Flyers (advertisement) | £ 950.00 |
| Books and Gifts | £ 650.00 |
| Hot Supper (soup and bread) for staff | £ 350.00 |
| **Total Expenditure** | **£10,700.00** |
| **Income - Expenditure** | **£0** |

*Note. It is vital that you set up a budget and have it voted at the Eldership Board, Church Board and Business/Members' meeting. This will avoid any future difficulties during the campaign. In addition, it is important to adjust the budget according to the income and expenditure. It may be necessary to increase the income from the church in areas where the Conference and others are unable to provide the full amount requested. Early submission to the Church and Conference will help in you realizing your budget.*

# THE EVANGELISTIC SERMON

*Preach the Word so that it will be easy to comprehend. Bring the people right to Jesus Christ, in whom their hopes of eternal life are centered. . . . As you bring to them the Word of God, presenting it in a simple style, the seed will grow, and after a time you will have a harvest. The seed sowing is your work; the propagation of the seed is the Lord's divine work. Letter 34, 1896. {Ev 178.3}*

# 4

## THE EVANGELISTIC SERMON
Excerpts from Burnett Robinson, Dynamic Evangelism and
Ellen G White, Evangelism

**The Sermon is the main feature of any campaign**. It reveals truths, exposes errors, comforts saints and conquers sinners. It is the means by which people are regenerated and faith generated in the area. Therefore, the sermon should be preached with power, fervour and dynamism.

At all times the business of a preacher/evangelist is not to amuse an audience with theatrical performances, but to cause it to muse. The only remedy for this poor sin-blasted, Satan-infested, proud, self sufficient and pleasure loving world is the gospel of God preached by a man of God in the spirit of God as he is constrained by the love of God. If Christ is lifted up, He will draw all people to Him.

**A sermon is more than a lecture/presentation**, or the development of some theological thought. A sermon is the outflow of life. It must pass through the crucible of your own soul, for it is only when this happens can it be a sermon of power. Sermons must not be few and should be new, they must be revised, upgraded and updated, never use those "found on the Internet or sermon banks."

**An evangelistic sermon** must be thought out before it's wrought out, it must be clear before it can be convincing. Don't be a story teller, be a Bible preacher, an expositor of the Word of God.

SERMON

In the presentation of your sermons, there are four things to guard against:

1. Being the shadow of another preacher. Be yourself.
2. A preacher's throat: You can't afford to have permanent laryngitis.
3. A poor vocabulary.
4. Avoid verbosity, remember Jesus' presentations were simple, clear, plain, but pinpointed.

Jesus' power was not in simple thinking, but in simple telling. His thoughts were profound. There should be windows in your sermons, windows that can give light and inspiration. The use of true illustrations, poems, quotations, and personal experiences, will edify the hearers and arrest their attention.

**As an evangelistic preacher,** never forget that you are not a preacher of reform but a preacher of redemption. "We are not sent to preach sociology, but salvation. Not economics, but evangelism. Not reform, but redemption. Not cultures, but conversion. Not progress, but pardoning of sins."

**Simple Speech; Clarity of Expression**. The Lord wishes you to learn how to use the gospel net. Many need to learn this art. In order for you to be successful in your work, the meshes of your net- the application of the Scriptures-must be close, and the meaning easily discerned. Then make the most of drawing in the net. Come right to the point. Make your illustrations self-evident. However great a man's knowledge, it is of no avail unless he is able to communicate it to others. Let the pathos of your voice, its deep feeling, make its impression on hearts. Urge your students to surrender themselves to God.

**Make your explanations clea**r; for I know that there are many who do not understand many of the things said to them. Let the Holy Spirit mold and fashion your speech, cleansing it from all dross. Speak as to little children, remembering that

SERMON

there are many well advanced in years who are but little children in understanding.

By earnest prayer and diligent effort we are to obtain a fitness for speaking. This fitness includes uttering every syllable clearly, placing the force and emphasis where it belongs. Speak slowly. Many speak rapidly, hurrying one word after another so fast that the effect of what they say is lost. Into what you say put the spirit and life of Christ. . . . To those who hear, the gospel is made the power of God unto salvation. Present the gospel in its simplicity.

**Attention to Sermon Preparation**. The discourses given upon present truth are full of important matter, and if these discourses are carefully considered before being presented to the people, if they are condensed and do not cover too much ground, if the spirit of the Master goes with the utterances, no one will be left in darkness, no one will have cause to complain of being unfed. The preparation, both in preacher and hearer, has very much to do with the result.

**Guard Spiritual Digestion.** "I do not like to go much beyond the half hour," said a faithful and earnest preacher, who certainly never gave to his hearers that which cost him nothing in the preparation. "I know that the spiritual digestion of some is but weak, and I should be sorry for my hearers to spend the second half hour in forgetting what I had said in the first, or in wishing that I would cease when I had given them as much as they could carry away."

**Cut Down Your Lengthy Discourses**. Some of your lengthy discourses would have far better effect upon the people if cut up into three. The people cannot digest so much; their minds cannot even grasp it, and they become wearied and confused by having so much matter brought before them in one discourse. Two thirds of such long discourses are lost, and the

SERMON

preacher is exhausted. There are many of our ministers who err in this respect. The result upon them is not good; for they become brain weary and feel that they are carrying heavy loads for the Lord and having a hard time.

The truth is so different in character and work from the errors preached from popular pulpits that when it is brought before the people for the first time, it almost overwhelms them. It is strong meat and should be dealt out judiciously. While some minds are quick to catch an idea, others are slow to comprehend new and startling truths which involve great changes and present a cross at every step. Give them time to digest the wonderful truths of the message you bear them.

The preacher should endeavor to carry the understanding and sympathies of the people with them. Do not soar too high, where they cannot follow, but give the truth point after point, slowly and distinctly, making a few essential points, then it will be as a nail fastened in a sure place by the Master of assemblies. If you stop when you should, giving them no more at once than they can comprehend and profit by, they will be eager to hear more, and thus the interest will be sustained.

## Types of Sermons

There are several types and forms of sermons. However, the type best suited for campaigns is that of Expository Doctrinal sermons. Expositions is where the specific Bible passage (pericope) is fully explained and applied in providing the necessary information relating to the doctrinal belief being preached (for example, Exodus 16:16-30 - The Sabbath and Faith in God's provision).

Doctrinal, where all of the basic textual evidence that deals with a specific truth found in the Bible are compared, compiled, examined and presented in light of the pericope and the plan of salvation (the bigger picture).

## There are two categories of doctrines

**1. Primary Doctrines**: These are Biblio-centric:

| | | | |
|---|---|---|---|
| a | Inspiration of the Bible | b | Steps in Salvation |
| c | Non immortality of the soul | d | Infallibility of the Law |
| e | Sabbath | f | Tithing |
| g | Gift of Prophecy | h | Second coming of Christ and related events |
| i | Baptism | j | Judgment |
| k | Temperance | l | Trinity |

**2. Secondary Doctrines:** These are community-centred
    a. Vegetarianism
    b. Dress (lipstick, earrings, rings...)

**Evangelistic sermons** are where a composite collection of all the basic sermons types and forms are preached motivate men and women to make positive decisions to:

1. Accept Jesus Christ as Saviour from the guilt, power and presence of sin
2. Accept the doctrines and teachings of Christ as the vehicle of salvation
3. Publicly express that commitment through baptism and to unite with Christ's visible body in the remnant church.

### Subject matters for the Evangelistic Sermon
1. Christ crucified for our sins
2. Christ risen from the dead
3. Christ our intercessor before God
4. Office work of the Holy Spirit
5. The Second Coming of Christ
6. Christ's personal dignity
7. Prophecies of Christ as the true Messiah
8. Christ's divinity
9. God's grace

All the above should be preached before acid (testing) doctrines are presented.

## Characteristic of the Sermon

Simple and short, not exceeding forty (40) minutes including appeal.
1. Lengthy sermons tax the strength of the preacher and the patience of the hearers.
2. Christ-Centred presentations
3. Clearly understandable
4. Not too much material
5. Preach affirmatively, positively and powerfully
6. Make appeal after every sermon. A good sermon that lacks a good appeal is a failure. Appeal is an art that must be developed. The only way to overcome the fear of making appeals is to make appeals. Make an appeal after every presentation.

## Ways of Response to an Appeal

1. Raising of the hand
2. Standing
3. Coming to the altar- use infrequently
4. Card signing
5. Turn in baptismal tags

Appeal not only to your visitors. Remember the meetings are for everyone. It is intended to strengthen members, reclaim backsliders and to proselyte to "The Truth." Appeals should not exceed ten (10) minutes.

## Guideline in Presenting Testing Doctrines
*Lift up Christ, for if He is lifted up, He will draw all men unto Him.*

The truths that normally cause adverse reactions in a campaign are:
1. The Law
2. The Sabbath
3. The State of the Dead

The difficulty is normally in order of outline. What should the Evangelist do?
1. Never present them until you ensure that there has been a level of conversion.
2. Softening messages should be presented as those mentioned earlier. These will stir the emotions and make it easier to appeal to the hearers.
3. Whatever the doctrine, Christ must be the theme. If it is the Sabbath, He is Lord of the Sabbath, if it is the State of the Dead; He is the resurrection and the life.

SERMON

# Spirit and Manner of Presenting
# The Message
Excerpts from Ellen G. White, Evangelism.

*The following excerpts, taken from the writings of Ellen White, are specifically chosen to assist presenters, lay preachers, lay evangelists and ministry leaders, as they prepare to present the gospel to those who do not know Christ and are not living in harmony with the Scriptures.*

**Importance of the Manner of Presenting Truth.** The manner in which the truth is presented often has much to do in determining whether it will be accepted or rejected.

It is to be regretted that many do not realize that the manner in which Bible truth is presented has much to do with the impressions made upon minds, and with the Christian character afterward developed by those who receive the truth. Instead of imitating Christ in His manner of labour, many are severe, critical, and dictatorial. They repulse instead of winning souls. Such will never know how many weak ones their harsh words have wounded and discouraged.

**Startling Messages.** Most startling messages will be borne by men of God's appointment, messages of a character to warn the people, to arouse them. And while some will be provoked by the warning, and led to resist light and evidence, we are to see from this that we are giving the testing message for this time. . . . We must also have, in our cities, consecrated evangelists through whom a message is to be borne so decidedly as to startle the hearers.

**With Certainty and Decision.** There is a living power in truth, and the Holy Spirit is the agent that opens human minds to the truth. But the ministers and workers who proclaim the truth must show certainty and decision. They are to go forth in faith, and present the Word as though they believed it. Try to make those for whom you labour understand that it is God's truth. Preach Jesus Christ and Him crucified. This will confront Satan's lies.

**The Word of the Living God.** If your way of presenting the truth is God's way, your audience will be deeply impressed with the truth you present. The conviction will come to them that it is the word of the living God, and you will accomplish the will of God in power.

**Big Ideas of Scripture Truth**. You do not present yourself, but the presence and preciousness of truth is so large, why, it is so far-reaching, so deep, so broad, that self is lost sight of. Preach so that the people can catch hold of big ideas and dig out the precious ones hid in the Scriptures.

**Meetings to Witness Deep Movings of Spirit**. At our meetings held in the cities, and at our camp meetings, we do not ask for great demonstrations, but we ask that the men who come before the people to present the truth shall be in earnest, and shall reveal that God is with them. There must be a special seeking after God, that the work of the meeting may be carried on under the deep movings of the Holy Spirit. There must be no mingling of the wrong with the right.

**More Activity and Zeal.** We need to break up the monotony of our religious labour. We are doing a work in the world, but we are not showing enough activity and zeal. If we were more in earnest, men would be convinced of the truth of our message. The tameness and monotony of our service for God repels many who are looking to see in us a deep, earnest, sanctified zeal. Legal religion will not answer for this age. We may perform all the outward acts of service, and yet be as destitute of the quickening influence of the Holy Spirit as the hills of Gilboa were destitute of dew and rain. We need spiritual mois-

SERMON

ture; and we need also the bright beams of the Sun of Righteousness to soften and subdue our hearts.

**Calm, Earnest Reasoning.** This is not excitement we wish to create, but deep, earnest consideration, that those who hear shall do solid work, real, sound, genuine work that will be enduring as eternity. We hunger not for excitement, for the sensational; the less we have of this, the better. The calm, earnest reasoning from the Scriptures is precious and fruitful. Here is the secret of success, in preaching a living personal Saviour in so simple and earnest a manner that the people may be able to lay hold by faith of the power of the Word of life.

**Present the Evidences of Truth.** People cannot be expected to see at once the advantage of truth over the error they have cherished. The best way to expose the fallacy of error is to present the evidences of truth. This is the greatest rebuke that can be given to error. Dispel the cloud of darkness resting on minds by reflecting the bright light of the Sun of Righteousness.

**Win Confidence of the People.** Those who labour for Christ should be men and women of great discretion, so that those who do not understand their doctrines may be led to respect them, and regard them as persons void of fanaticism, void of rashness and impetuosity. Their discourses and conduct and conversation should be of a nature that will lead men to the conclusion that these ministers are men of thought, of solidity of character, men who fear and love their Heavenly Father. They should win the confidence of the people, so that those who listen to the preaching may know that the ministers have not come with some cunningly devised fable, but that their words are words of worth, a testimony that demands thought and attention. Let the people see you exalting Jesus, and hiding self.

**No Long, Far-fetched, Complicated Reasoning.** Christ seldom attempted to prove that truth is truth. He illustrated truth in all its bearings, and then left His hearers free to accept or reject it, as they might choose. He did not force anyone to believe. In the sermon on the mount He instructed the people in practical godliness, distinctly outlining their duty. He spoke in such a manner as to commend truth to the conscience. The power manifested by the disciples was revealed in the clearness and earnestness with which they expressed the truth.

In Christ's teaching there is no long, far-fetched, complicated reasoning. He comes right to the point. In His ministry He read every heart as an open book, and from the inexhaustible store of His treasure house He drew things both new and old to illustrate and enforce His teachings. He touched the heart, and awakened the sympathies.

**Simple, Forcible Doctrinal Teaching.** A few forcible remarks upon some point of doctrine will fasten it in the mind much more firmly than if such a mass of matter were presented that nothing lies out clear and distinct in the mind of those ignorant of our faith. There should be interspersed with the prophecies practical lessons of the teachings of Christ.

**God Will Give Fit Words.** What a privilege it is to labour for the conversion of souls! Our calling is high. . . . To fit us to do this work, He will strengthen our mental faculties as verily as He did the mind of Daniel. As we teach those in darkness to understand the truths that have enlightened us, God will teach us to understand these truths still better ourselves. He will give us apt words to speak, communicating to us through the angel standing by our side.

**Less Controversy-More of Christ.** We need far less controversy, and far more presentation of Christ. Our Redeemer is the center of all our faith and hope. Those who can present

His matchless love, and inspire hearts to give Him their best and holiest affections, are doing work that is great and holy. The many argumentative sermons preached seldom soften and subdue the soul.

**Do Not Rail.** Those who advocate the truth can afford to be fair and pleasant. It does not need the human mixing in. It is not for you to use the Holy Spirit of God, but it is for the Holy Spirit to use you. Be careful that you do not rail once. We want the Holy Spirit of God to be life and voice for us. Our tongue should be as the pen of a ready writer, because the Spirit of God is speaking through the human agent. When you use that twit and fling, you have stirred in some of yourself, and we do not want anything of that mixture.

**Do Not Attack Authorities.** Our work is not to make a raid on the Government but to prepare a people to stand in the great day of the Lord. The fewer attacks we make on authorities and powers, the more work will we do for God. While the truth must be defended, this work is to be done in the spirit of Jesus. If God's people work without peace and love, they work at a great loss, an irretrievable loss. Souls are driven from Christ even after they have been connected with His work.

We are not to pass judgment on those who have not had the opportunities and privileges we have had. Some of these will go into heaven before those who have had great light but have not lived up to the light. If we wish to convince unbelievers that we have the truth that sanctifies the soul and transforms the character, we must not vehemently charge them with their errors. Thus we force them to the conclusion that the truth does not make us kind and courteous, but coarse and rough. Some, easily excited, are always ready to take up the weapons of warfare. In times of trial they will show that they have not founded their faith on the solid rock.

Let Seventh-day Adventists do nothing that will mark them

SERMON

as lawless and disobedient. Let them keep all inconsistency out of their lives. Our work is to proclaim the truth, leaving the issues with the Lord. Do all in your power to reflect the light, but do not speak words that will irritate or provoke.

**Presenting Truth in Fierce Way**. In the past you have presented the truth in a fierce way, using it as if it were a scourge. This has not glorified the Lord. You have given the people the rich treasures of God's Word, but your manner has been so condemnatory that they have turned from them. You have not taught the truth in the way that Christ taught it. You present it in a way that mars its influence. . . . Your heart needs to be filled with the converting grace of Christ.

**Present the Truth Tenderly.** Let every minister learn to wear the gospel shoes. He who is shod with the preparation of the gospel of peace will walk as Christ walked. He will be able to speak right words, and to speak them in love. He will not try to drive home God's message of truth. He will deal tenderly with every heart, realizing that the Spirit will impress the truth on those who are susceptible to divine impressions. Never will he be vehement in his manner. Every word spoken will have a softening, subduing influence.

In speaking words of reproof, let us put all the Christlike tenderness and love possible into the voice. The higher a minister's position, the more circumspect should he be in word and act.

**Reclaim Rather Than Condemn.** All whose hearts are in sympathy with the heart of Infinite Love will seek to reclaim, and not to condemn. Christ dwelling in the soul is a spring that never runs dry. Where He abides, there will be an overflowing of beneficence.

**Apply Truth to Heart.** In every address given, let there be an application of truth to the heart, that whosoever may hear shall understand, and that men, women, and youth may become alive unto God.

**Easy to Comprehend.** Preach the Word so that it will be easy to comprehend. Bring the people right to Jesus Christ, in whom their hopes of eternal life are centered. . . . As you bring to them the Word of God, presenting it in a simple style, the seed will grow, and after a time you will have a harvest. The seed sowing is your work; the propagation of the seed is the Lord's divine work.

**Practical Godliness in Every Discourse.** It is harder to reach the hearts of men today than it was twenty years ago. The most convincing arguments may be presented, and yet sinners seem as far from salvation as ever. Ministers should not preach sermon after sermon on doctrinal subjects alone. Practical godliness should find a place in every discourse.

**Preach Realties of the Message.** On a certain occasion, when Betterton, the celebrated actor, was dining with Dr. Sheldon, Archbishop of Canterbury, the Archbishop said to him, "Pray, Mr. Betterton, tell me why it is that you actors affect your audiences so powerfully by speaking of things imaginary." "My lord," replied Betterton, "with due submission to Your Grace, permit me to say that the reason is plain; it all lies in the power of enthusiasm. We on the stage speak of things imaginary as if they were real; and you in the pulpit speak of things real as if they were imaginary."

**No Compromise.** We are not to cringe and beg pardon of the world for telling them the truth: we should scorn concealment. Unfurl your colors to meet the cause of men and angels. Let it be understood that Seventh-day Adventists can make no compromise. In your opinions and faith there must not be the least appearance of wavering: the world has a right to know what to expect of us.

**Our World-wide Message**. We are one in faith in the fundamental truths of God's Word. . . . We have a world-wide message. The commandments of God and the testimonies of Jesus Christ are the burden of our work.

**Preaching for a Revival**. Repent, repent, was the message rung out by John the Baptist in the wilderness. Christ's message to the people was, "Except ye repent, ye shall all likewise perish." Luke 13:5. And the apostles were commanded to preach everywhere that men should repent.

The Lord desires His servants today to preach the old gospel doctrine, sorrow for sin, repentance, and confession. We want old-fashioned sermons, old-fashioned customs, old-fashioned fathers and mothers in Israel. The sinner must be laboured for, perseveringly, earnestly, wisely, until he shall see that he is a transgressor of God's law, and shall exercise repentance toward God and faith toward the Lord Jesus Christ.

**Comforting, Powerful Preaching.** You should have a clear apprehension of the gospel. The religious life is not one of gloom and of sadness but of peace and joy coupled with Christlike dignity and holy solemnity. We are not encouraged by our Saviour to cherish doubts and fears and distressing forebodings; these bring no relief to the soul and should be rebuked rather than praised. We may have joy unspeakable and full of glory. Let us put away our indolence and study God's Word more constantly. If we ever needed the Holy Ghost to be with us, if we ever needed to preach in the demonstration of the Spirit, it is at this very time.

**A Cheerful Present-Truth Message.** Now, just now, we are to proclaim present truth, with assurance and with power. Do not strike one dolorous note; do not sing funeral hymns.

SERMON

# Song Evangelism

Excerpts from Ellen G. White, Evangelism.

## The Ministry of Song

**A Soul-saving Instrumentality.** The melody of song, poured forth from many hearts in clear, distinct utterance, is one of God's instrumentalities in the work of saving souls.

**The Power of Song.** As the children of Israel, journeying through the wilderness cheered their way by the music of sacred song, so God bids His children today gladden their pilgrim life. There are few means more effective for fixing His words in the memory than repeating them in song. And such song has wonderful power. It has power to subdue rude and uncultivated natures; power to quicken thought and to awaken sympathy, to promote harmony of action, and to banish the gloom and foreboding that destroy courage and weaken effort.

It is one of the most effective means of impressing the heart with spiritual truth. How often to the soul hard-pressed and ready to despair, memory recalls some word of God's-the long forgotten burden of a childhood song-and temptations lose their power, life takes on new meaning and new purpose, and courage and gladness are imparted to other souls.

**A Continual Sermon.** These words [song of Moses] were repeated unto all Israel, and formed a song, which was often sung, poured forth in exalted strains of melody. This was the wisdom of Moses to present the truth to them in song, that in strains of melody they should become familiar with them, and be impressed upon the minds of the whole nation, young and old. It was important for the children to learn the song; for this would speak to them, to warn, to restrain, to reprove, and encourage.

**Far-reaching Influence.** The service of song was made a regular part of religious worship, and David composed psalms, not only for the use of the priests in the sanctuary service, but also to be sung by the people in their journeys to the national altar at the annual feasts. The influence thus exerted was far-reaching, and it resulted in freeing the nation from idolatry. Many of the surrounding peoples, beholding the prosperity of Israel, were led to think favourably of Israel's God, who had done such great things for His people.

**A Connecting Link With God.** There must be a living connection with God in prayer, a living connection with God in songs of praise and thanksgiving.

**To Resist the Enemy.** When Christ was a child like these children here, He was tempted to sin, but He did not yield to temptation. As He grew older He was tempted, but the songs His mother had taught Him to sing came into His mind, and He would lift His voice in praise. And before His companions were aware of it, they would be singing with Him. God wants us to use every facility, which Heaven has provided for resisting the enemy.

**Bringing Heaven's Gladness.** The early morning often found Him in some secluded place, meditating, searching the Scriptures, or in prayer. With the voice of singing He welcomed the morning light. Songs of thanksgiving He cheered His hours of labour, and brought heaven's gladness to the toil-worn and disheartened.

**The Song of Praise.** Often He expressed the gladness of His heart by singing psalms and heavenly songs. Often the dwellers in Nazareth heard His voice rose in praise and thanksgiving to God. He held communion with heaven in song; and as His companions complained of weariness from labour, they were cheered by the sweet melody from His lips. His praise

SONG

71

seemed to banish the evil angels, and, like incense, fill the place with fragrance. The minds of His hearers were carried away from their earthly exile, to the heavenly home.

## *Music in Evangelism*

**To Impress Spiritual Truth**. Song is one of the most effective means of impressing spiritual truth upon the heart. Often by the words of sacred song, the springs of penitence and faith have been unsealed.

**Musical Instruments**. Let the talent of singing be brought into the work. The use of musical instruments is not at all objectionable. There were used in religious services in ancient times. The worshipers praised God upon the harp and cymbal, and music should have its place in our services. It will add to the interest.

**The Theme of Every Song.** The science of salvation is to be the burden of every sermon, the theme of every song. Let it be poured forth in every supplication.

**Calling for Decisions in Song.** In my dreams last night I was speaking to a company of young men. I asked them to sing "Almost Persuaded." Some present were deeply moved. I knew that they were almost persuaded, but that if they did not make decided efforts to return to Christ, the conviction of their sinfulness would leave them. You made some confessions, and I asked you, "Will you not from this time stand on the Lord's side?" If you will receive Jesus, He will receive you.

SONG

## The Power of Song
Excerpt from Ellen White, Education, 167-168

The history of the songs of the Bible is full of suggestion as to the uses and benefits of music and song. Music is often perverted to serve purposes of evil, and it thus becomes one of the most alluring agencies of temptation. But, rightly employed, it is a precious gift of God, designed to uplift the thoughts to high and noble themes, to inspire and elevate the soul.

### A Weapon Against Discouragement

If there was much more praising the Lord, and far less doleful recitation of discouragements, many more victories would be achieved.  Let praise and thanksgiving be expressed in song. When tempted, instead of giving utterance to our feelings, let us by faith lift up a song of thanksgiving to God (White, Letter 53, 1896; Evangelism, 499.)

Song is a weapon that we can always use against discouragement. As we thus open the heart to the sunlight of the Saviour's presence, we shall have health and His blessing (White, Ministry of Healing, 1905, 254.)

**To Impress Spiritual Truth**. Song is one of the most effective means of impressing spiritual truth upon the heart. Often by the words of sacred song, the springs of penitence and faith have been unsealed (White, Review and Herald, June 6, 1912.) If it was essential for Moses to embody the commandments in sacred song, so that as they marched in the wilderness, the children could learn to sing the law verse by verse, how essential it is at this time teach our children God's Word (White, Evangelism, 499.)

SONG

## *Music That Offends God*

Display is not religion nor sanctification. There is nothing more offensive in God's sight than a display of instrumental music when those taking part are not consecrated, are not making melody in their hearts to the Lord. The offering most sweet and acceptable in God's sight is a heart made humble by self-denial, by lifting the cross and following Jesus. We have no time now to spend in seeking these things that only please the senses. Close heart searching is needed. With tears and heartbroken confession we need to draw nigh to God that He may draw nigh to us (White, Evangelism, 510.)

## The Singing Evangelist

**Preparing for Song Evangelism**. There should be much more interest in voice culture than is now generally manifested. Students who have learned to sing sweet gospel songs with melody and distinctness can do much good as singing evangelists. They will find many opportunities to use the talent that God has given them, carrying melody and sunshine into many lonely places darkened by sin and sorrow and affliction, singing to those who seldom have church privileges.

**A Power to Win Souls.** There is great pathos and music in the human voice, and if the learner will make determined efforts, he will acquire habits of talking and singing that will be to him a power to win souls to Christ.

**Bearing a Special Message in Song.** There are those who have a special gift of song, and there are times when a special message is borne by one singing alone or by several uniting in song. But the singing is seldom to be done by a few. The ability to sing is a talent of influence, which God desires all to cultivate and use to His name's glory.

**Clear Intonations-Distinct Utterance.** No words can properly set forth the deep blessedness of genuine worship. When human beings sing with the Spirit and the understanding, heavenly musicians take up the strain, and join in the song of thanksgiving. He who has bestowed upon us all the gifts that enable us to be workers together with God, expects His servants to cultivate their voices, so that they can speak and sing in a way that all can understand. It is not loud singing that is needed, but clear intonation, correct pronunciation, and distinct utterance. Let all take time to cultivate the voice, so that God's praise can be sung in clear, soft tones, not with harshness and shrillness that offend the ear. The ability to sing is the gift of God; let it be used to His glory.

**Factors in Effectual Music.** Music can be a great power for good; yet we do not make the most of this branch of worship. The singing is generally done from impulse or to meet special cases, and at other times those who sing are left to blunder along, and the music loses its proper effect upon the minds of those present. Music should have beauty, pathos, and power. Let the voices be lifted in songs of praise and devotion. Call to your aid, if practicable, instrumental music, and let the glorious harmony ascend to God, an acceptable offering.

But it is sometimes more difficult to discipline the singers and keep them in working order, than to improve the habits of praying and exhorting. Many want to do things after their own style; they object to consultation, and are impatient under leadership. Well-matured plans are needed in the service of God. Common sense is an excellent thing in the worship of the Lord.

**The Heavenly Song Director.** I have been shown the order, the perfect order, of heaven, and have been enraptured as I listened to the perfect music there. After coming out of vision, the singing here has sounded very harsh and discordant. I have seen companies of angels, who stood in a hollow

SONG

square, everyone having a harp of gold. There is one angel who always leads, who first touches the harp and strikes the note, and then all join in the rich, perfect music of heaven. It cannot be described. It is melody; heavenly, divine, while from every countenance beams the image of Jesus, shining with glory unspeakable.

**A Well-directed Song Program.** A minister should not give out hymns to be sung until it has first been ascertained that they are familiar to those who sing. A proper person should be appointed to take charge of this exercise, and it should be his duty to see that such hymns are selected as can be sung with the spirit and with the understanding also. Singing is a part of the worship of God, but in the bungling manner in which it is often conducted, it is no credit to the truth, and no honor to God. There should be system and order in this as well as every other part of the Lord's work. Organize a company of the best singers, whose voices can lead the congregation, and then let all who will, unite with them. Those who sing should make an effort to sing in harmony; they should devote some time to practice, that they may employ this talent to the glory of God. But singing should not be allowed to divert the mind from the hours of devotion. If one must be neglected, let it be the singing.

## The Music Personnel

In their efforts to reach the people, the Lord's messengers are not to follow the ways of the world. In the meetings that are held, they are not to depend on worldly singers and theatrical display to awaken an interest. How can those who have no interest in the Word of God, who have never read His Word with a sincere desire to understand its truths, be expected to sing with the spirit and the understanding? How can their hearts be in harmony with the words of sacred song? How can the heavenly choir join in music that is only a form?

**Worldly Musicians.** Do not hire worldly musicians if this can possibly be avoided. Gather together singers who will sing with the spirit and with the understanding also. The extra display which you sometimes make entails unnecessary expense, which the brethren should not be asked to meet; and you will find that after a time unbelievers will not be willing to give money to meet these expenses.

**Accepting Musical Help Offered**. In the meetings held the singing should not be neglected. God can be glorified by this part of the service. And when singers offer their services, they should be accepted. But money should not be used to hire singers. Often the singing of simple hymns by the congregation has a charm that is not possessed by the singing of a choir, however skilled it may be.

SONG

# TRAINING LIGHT BEARERS

*Suggestions on Preparing a Bible Study*

*The disciples of Christ are required to represent their Lord to the world. They have been set as torch-bearers on the road to heaven. The light is not given to any soul to be put under a bushel, or under the bed; but to be put on a candlestick, that it may give light to all that are in the house. The lower lights must be kept burning. Jesus is the great light which lights up every man that comes into the world. All heaven is interested in the conflict that is going on in this world between truth and error, light and darkness. The great Source of all light is constantly shining, and those who will catch His rays, and will reflect them upon others, will be light-bearers in this darkened world.*

# 5

# TRAINING LIGHT BEARERS
*Suggestions on Preparing a Bible Study*

The following practical suggestions in seeking to prepare a Bible study:

**1. Decide Upon Your Subject.** First, decided definitely what you are to talk about. Haziness as to the theme will mean haziness all through the study. The selection of your subject may be determined by three things: (a) the needs of the hearers, (b) respect to the proper sequence of thought, (c) the occasion. You should endeavour to know the spiritual needs of your hearers and the extent of their knowledge of the Bible. Then you should pray earnestly for the direction of God's Spirit as to how to supply the need. Sequence of thought should be considered in giving a series of studies, that there may be the proper arrangement of topics and correct order of development.

**2. Gather Suitable Bible texts.** Having decided upon the subject, your next procedure is that of the gathering of texts. First, jot down any texts that may come to your mind as bearing on the subject. Thoughts may occur at any time, so it is well to jot them down when they occur; otherwise they may be lost. When you have exhausted your own resources you may add to your list by using the concordance, looking up words likely to be contained in Scripture and also connected with the theme. It may be advisable to consult a book on Bible doctrines to see whether any important texts have been omitted. In securing your material, make no attempt to classify the texts, but write a brief thought beside each, suggestive of the leading thought or of the purpose for which the text could be used.

**3. Build Your Framework.** Now that the material is collected, you are ready to build. The first part of the study to be constructed will be the framework, and the material before us will suggest the kind of framework to erect. This framework will consist of suitable heads to mark the division of the study. These divisions should give the main points to be developed in the study, and should be stated concisely and clearly. As to the number of headings in a study, there is no definite rule, except the fewer the better. Three or four is a good number. Endeavour to classify them in such a way as to show a definite relationship to one another and to the theme. For instance, in a study on the Second Advent you could make an outline that reflects the theme.

*Theme: The Second Coming of Christ*

**Division:**

1. The promise of Christ's return,
2. The manner of Christ's return,
3. The time of Christ's return,
4. The purpose of Christ's return

**After erecting the framework of your study,** begin the work of building the needed texts into their proper places. It is not necessary to use all the texts that have been gathered. This would usually make the study too long (always remember to stick to the agreed start and finish time. This will be make it a lot easier for your hearers to schedule more studies as they know they can count on you starting and finishing on time without jeopardizing their other activities). Therefore use only those texts best suited to the theme. Always aim at the selection of simple texts that state specifically just what you wish to present. It would be better to leave out of the study any text that requires a lengthy explanation. A common mistake, especially among beginners, is to put too much into one study. Nothing is gained by overfeeding with even the best of food, and it is better to divide the subject into two, rather than to give more on one occasion than the mind is able to receive. Aim at teaching three or four points thoroughly in each study, and your work will achieve far better results.

**One text, as a rule, is quite sufficient to prove a point.** It only amounts to a weakness to keep hammering away at a point once it has been proved. Nothing is gained by continuing to hit the nail on the head when once it has been driven home. *Ask what is learnt at the end of each study*

### Seven Rules Suggested

1.  **Use the most convincing text first**. A first impression is always the strongest, and the most likely to become permanent. Prove your point at the start, and the battle is more than half won.

2.  **Use no expression or text too hard to comprehend.** Truth shines, and its rays, shining into the heart darkened by sin, convert. But in spiritual things the natural heart is slow of comprehension; so in presenting truth use simple forms of speech, and select texts that, on their face, clearly state just what you claim. At least, avoid more obscure texts until your listeners have become wise in spiritual research and able to digest the strong meat of the Word.

3.  **Use as few questions as possible.** Six or seven questions during a study are usually sufficient. As a general rule it is advisable to restrict the study to about forty-five  minutes (45minutes) period.

4.  **In answering your own questions, use few words**. The questions here meant are those found in the

LIGHTBEARERS

study which are to be answered by texts from the Bible. Be brief in all that you present to your hearers. The power is in the Word of God. Use just enough words to make the principles of truth shine out clearly; then let the convincing power of the Spirit do the rest.

5.  **To end the study, use a text that clinches the points made in the study**. Leave nothing for the people to guess at, and about which it is possible to come to wrong conclusions. Finish the subject before you leave it, so that the hearers may be able to trace it out for themselves. Prove fully what you set out to prove at the beginning. Awaken interest in the next study by announcing the subject.

6.  **Let every question be so stated that the chosen text will answer it.** Ask no question that requires a reply in your own words. Always let the Bible answer the question; otherwise the people will begin to say, "that's what you say, not what the Bible teaches." Your statement will not carry conviction; that power is in the Word.

*[handwritten margin note: Ask questions where the bible gives answers?]*

7.  **Use, preferable,** but one text to answer a question. Avoid all complications. The aim should be to help the listener to store up the statements of truth presented. A superfluity of evidence tends to mental confusion. Usually one text is sufficient to answer a question.

### Helps in Preparing a Bible Study

The tools required by the lay work person for God are not numerous, but each is essential to success:

1.  **A reference Bible.** This is the chief tool of the Bible instructor and should be chosen for lifetime use. It should be of medium size with clear type and sub-

stantial binding. **Markings and notations that are added from time to time make this particular Bible preferable to all others,** as one becomes familiar with its pages and the location of special texts for ready reference.

2. **A concordance.** There are several to be commended: Cruden's or Walker's will serve to good purpose

3. **Books, loose**-leaf doctrinal studies, and periodicals
   a. Studying Together, by Mark Finley
   b. Bible Lessons for Catholics, by Mary Walsh
   c. The Seventh-day Adventist Believes-
      Fundamental beliefs
   d. The Fundamental of the Seventh-day Adventist Church

*Read*

# Order of Subjects
# To follow the Evangelistic Series

**The series of subjects** and the order of presentations are matters of vital importance. While it is understood that in the majority of cases the giving of Bible studies by the laity is on a more irregular basis that the work done by the full-time conference Bible instructor, yet the blending of subjects in proper order and in abbreviated form, adapted to the situation, requires due consideration by those who would "act their part, doing house-to-house work and giving Bible readings in families."

No hard and fast rule can be laid down for the proper order of subjects. A great deal depends on the mental attitude of the person following the studies as well as on the judgment of the one conducting them. In this matter the Holy Spirit should be allowed to guide in a very definite way. However, there are logical arrangements of subjects that

**LIGHTBEARERS**

have been prepared by experienced Bible teachers, and these may well serve as a guide for study and adaptation:

1. The word of God
2. Daniel, Second Chapter
3. Second Coming of Christ
4. Signs of Christ's Coming
5. The Millennium
6. Destiny of the Wicked
7. Home of the Saved
8. Daniel 7 and the Little Horn
9. Christ Our High Priest
10. The Investigative Judgment
11. The Law and the Gospel
12. The Sabbath
13. The Sabbath and the New Testament
14. Origin of Sunday Observance
15. Seal of God and the Mark of the Beast
16. Origin of Evil Angels
17. The Nature of Man, State of the Dead
18. Spiritualism
19. Jesus Saves the Lost
20. Faith
21. God's True Church
22. The Ordinances of the Church
23. The Body Temple
24. Precious Promises
25. Work of the Holy Spirit
26. The Christian's Duty
27. Controversy Between Christ and Satan
28. Acceptable Prayer
29. The Ministry of Christ in Heaven
30. Growing In Christ

The reason for following the listed order of subjects is because it provides a clear pathway for those not familiar with the word of God to become acquainted and as well as to better understands the teachings of the Bible and the Seventh-

LIGHTBEARERS

day Adventist church. Therefore, the campaign is, in reality, a large bible study class.

Pastor Dwight Nelson, in the Next Millennium seminars, order of subject provides a good alternative for campaigns. This is useful where the audience has some knowledge of the word of God:

1. Introduction to Revelation
2. Origin of Sin and suffering
3. Ten Commandments
4. The Gospel
5. Salvation
6. Evolution vs. Creation
7. Sabbath
8. Change of the Sabbath- Biblical Look
9. Change of the Sabbath- Historical Look
10. Second Coming
11. Signs of the Times
12. State of the Dead
13. Hell
14. Judgment-Introduction
15. Judgment-Part 2
16. Baptism
17. Revelation 13
18. U.S. in Prophecy
19. Spiritism
20. 2300 Days Prophecy
21. The Fourth Commandment
22. True Church
23. Spirit of Prophecy
24. Stewardship
25. Christian Living
26. Heaven
27. Prayer and Devotions
28. Marriage
29. Health Message
30. The Remnant and Loyalty to God

# RESTRUCTURING THE PERSONAL MINISTRIES DEPARTMENT FOR EFFECTIVE EVANGELISTIC OUTREACH

*The central mission of the Seventh-day Adventist Church is to   fulfil the gospel commission, "Therefore go and make disciples of all nations, baptizing them in the name of the Father and of the Son and of the Holy Spirit" (Matthew 28:19).*

*Proposal for restructuring the Personal Ministries Department in the Local church for Effective Evangelism (Inreach for the ministry of winning, nurturing and training members for mission and ministries. Outreach coordinator for reaching out to the churches community without distracting from the nurturing needs of the members. Prison ministries, Community Care and Health Ministries to add to the Inreach and Outreach aspect of the church).*

## Evangelism Council-
Proposed

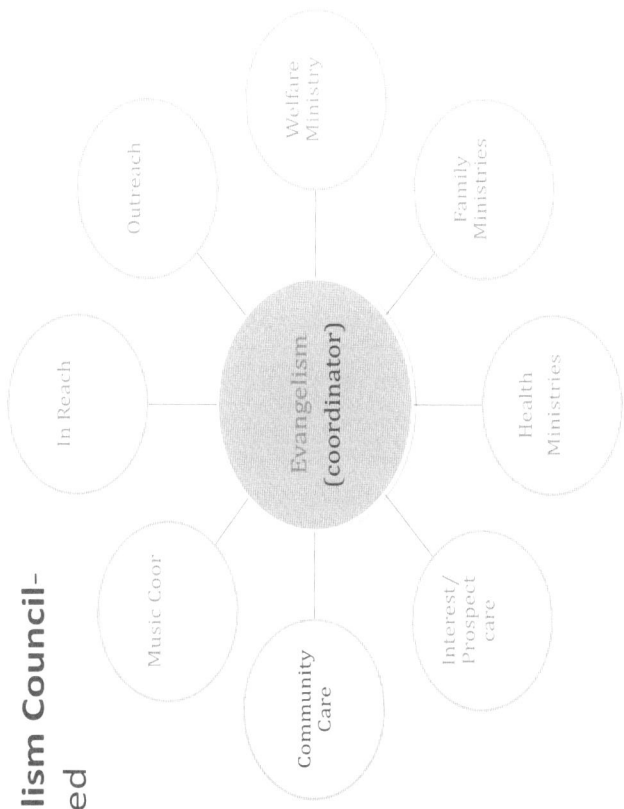

Evangelism
(coordinator)

Welfare Ministry

Family Ministries

Health Ministries

Interest/ Prospect care

Community Care

Music Coor

In Reach

Outreach

Illustration No.2

# 6

## GROWING THE CHURCH THROUGH STRATEGIC PLANNING

### Description of Strategic Planning

Monumental changes are taking place in the world and in the church. Because of this I believe a whole new way of reaching the church's community must be developed (Peter Brierley and Kim Miles, eds. 35-55.)   One suggested strategy is to use some of the characteristics of a healthy church as suggested by Christian A. Schwartz and Christoph Schalk, as a means of verifying the health of the church (Christian A Schwartz, and Christoph Schalk 15.)

Strategic planning is the process of determining a company's or an institution's long-term objectives, and ways to achieve those objectives.  It is a continual improvement process that effectively monitors performance against goals, analyses achievements and shortfalls, and adjusts activities to accomplish the desired results. Carter McNamara lists six things that need to be clarified in strategic planning: (1) the purpose, or mission, of the nonprofit organization, (2) the desired status, or vision, for the nonprofit (*in our context, this refers to the church*) and its clients at some point in the future, usually in the next one to three years, (3) how the nonprofit is going to achieve that status, including the analysing of the external and internal environments of the organization, establishing goals, implementing strategies to achieve the goals, and by operating according to certain overall priorities, or values, (4) action plans, including specifying who is going to be doing what and by when in order to implement the strategies, (5) what resources are needed in order to implement the strategies and action plans, including budgeting for those resources, such as people, materials, equipment, and facilities, and (6) how to make sure that an organization is on track to get there, including the implementation, monitoring and adjustment of the plans (Carter McNamara 3.)

Strategic planning serves a variety of purposes in an organization, such as:
(1) to clearly define the purpose of the organization and to establish realistic goals and objectives consistent with the mission and vision of the organization, (2) to communicate those goals and objectives to the organization's constituents, (3) to develop a sense of ownership of the plan, (4) to ensure the most effective use is made of the organization's resources by focusing the resources on the key priorities, and (5) to provide a base from which progress can be measured and establish a mechanism for informed changes when needed (Carter McNamara.)

## Tools for Strategic Planning

When developing a project plan (outreach, inreach or planning to revitalised the church), it is necessary to have action plans, a monitoring system, and a framework for evaluation. One of the best way to approach strategic planning is to use the Logical Framework Approach (LFA) to present the plan. The Logical Framework Approach is a way of presenting essential elements of a plan in a logical sequence, ensuring feasibility and sustainability. LFA is an useful tool in the design, planning, implementation, and monitoring of a project. It also makes it easier to report on a project, and highlights changes that need to be adapted (European Commission, 15.)

Planning for a project needs to be divided into two phases: (1) the analysis phase during which the church's situation is analysed in order to develop a vision of the future, and (2) the planning phase during which the project ideas will be developed in operational detail.

The basic components of a logframe are as follows:

1.  ***Overall Objectives***—The ultimate aim, which addresses the wider problem the plan will help to resolve, the plan can only hope to provide a partial solution, and thus the plan will not be expected to achieve the goal by itself, but will only make a contribution towards it.

2. ***Project Purpose***—The intended impact and outcome that a plan is intended to bring about, or the changes or benefits to be achieved by the plan; or the immediate impact on the project area or target group.

3. ***Outputs/Results***—The specific achievements, deliverable, or results of completed activities that when combined should bring about attainment of the objective/purpose.

4. ***Activities***—The tasks to be carried out, or work to be done, to translate inputs into outputs.

5. ***Assumptions***—These are conditions, which must be met if the project is to succeed. Assumptions made about the risks and critical factors necessary for a plan's success or the uncertainties which the plan will face during implementation.

6. ***Objectively Verifiable Indicators***—Ways of measuring or indicating that progress is being achieved, "Quantitative ways of measuring, or qualitative ways of judging, timed achievement of objective/production of outputs."

7. ***Sources of Verification***—The procedures for collecting information that will verify whether targets and estimates were reached or not or sources of proof which verify the achievement of the goal/objective/output indicators.

Table showing the Logical Framework (logframe) for a proposed project in the "X" Seventh-day Adventist Community Church.

| | Intervention Logic | Verifiable Indicators | Source of Verification | Assumptions |
|---|---|---|---|---|
| Overall Goal | A healthy Seventh-day Adventist Church | To improve by 5% each of the church's two minimum factors each year using the NCD analysis and checklists. | NCD profile surveys and checklists for ongoing check, annual reports | That NCD survey can suitably measure health in the Adventist church. |
| Project Purpose | Church displaying at least eight quality characteristics of the Natural Church Development (NCD) profile. | | | |
| Results/ Outputs | 1. Build Relationships with Other Members | Church to host at least one social event annually | Number of members attending social events | That people will attend events |
| | 2. Strengthen Relationships with Christ | 1. Increase tithe and offering annually by 5%. 2. Increase members' attendance at mid-week prayer meeting by 5% quarterly | 1. Attendance at Sabbath School 2. Attendance at the main worship service | That people will be open and will give testimonies during main services |
| | 3. Involve Church Members in Mission | 1. Increase Sabbath School attendance by 5% quarterly 2. Increase annual number of baptisms by 5% | 1. Baptism records 2. Number of Bible studies being given 3. Amount Of people giving Bible Studies | That members will take part in events and will keep a record of their activities and be willing to report It |

91

| | Intervention Logic | Verifiable Indicators | Source of Verification | Assumptions |
|---|---|---|---|---|
| | 4. Member Involvement in Ministry | Increase the number of people taking church offices by 2% annually | No. of members in office and working | |
| Activities | 1. Train members in how to establish and maintain relationships with others.<br>2. Develop and conduct seminars to strengthen members relationship with Christ.<br>3. Create opportunities for members to be involved in evangelistic events.<br>4. Provide training in servant leadership | (See activity and resource schedule) | | 1.Assuming that the church board will support the projects<br>2. Assuming the church will vote to undertake the project<br>3. Assuming that members will be willing to attend the seminars. |

## Advantages of a Logframe

The reason why a logframe model was chosen for this project is that it provides a pictorial, visual representation of the entire strategy. It points out areas of strength and/or weakness, and allows those benefiting from the project to run through the many possible scenarios to find the best possible solution (W. K. Kellogg Foundation 5.)

Another important reason is that the logframe matrix is able to show the relationship between cause and effect. It provides an analytical process and a way of presenting the results of this process, which makes it possible to set out systematically and logically the project's objectives and causal relationships.

Objective and impact focused planning makes people think through the logic and structure of a plan, can facilitate discussion, negotiation, agreement, consensus on the plan between different stakeholders, and can be used in conjunction with participatory tools like a problem tree for cause and effect, and for a clear and simple presentation of the plan. Poorly thought-out plans become easily apparent.

A logframe also causes people to think about how they will monitor and evaluate the program by identifying indicators at the start.

A logframe can also be used in evaluation by means of a verification column promoting realistic planning of cost-effective assessment goals and assumptions, ensuring that external factors are taken into account, and that the strategy is not too risky. If a logframe is used intelligently in a participatory team planning approach, it can undoubtedly be very useful to managers and staff in planning, monitoring, and evaluating their work. A logframe can also provide a clear, succinct, and logical presentation of a plan to other stakeholders.

# Strategy Development
# For "X" Seventh-day Adventist Church

The overall goal of the project for the "X" Seventh-day Adventist Church (XSDA) is to become a healthy and holistic church, thus being able to have an efficient ministry in the community (internal and external). By becoming healthy, the church will be able to impact its community and will eventually reflect the makeup of its location.

### Goals

The goal of this project is to have the church growing in a natural way, in accordance with the biblical mode of church growth, and following the eight characteristics that Christian Schwarz says are exhibited in growing churches and which he believes are the "key to their success." This project will employ the NCD surveys, church health analysis, and practical steps in developing a strategy for the "XSDA".

Each part in this plan is an essential component in the bigger goal of creating a community church that is able to do more than just preach the gospel. The church should be able to minister to the needs of its members, spiritually, socially, and physically. In addition, the training elements should provide both members and visitors with the necessary tools and information to grow spiritually and physically.

In this section, I have focused the project on one overall goal instead of several goals, in order that the purposes and the results will be achieved. In so doing, activities can be planned that contribute to the purpose, which in turn contribute to achieving the overall goal. The advantage of having a goal is that everyone can see what the strategy seeks to achieve. Without a goal the various purposes and activities become meaningless because there is no way of measuring outcomes or evaluating whether the problem or issue has been solved.

## Objectives

In order to know whether the project is achieving its goal, the logical framework approach uses objectively verifiable indicators (OVI) that are "ways of measuring (indicating) that progress is being achieved." OVIs describe the project's objectives in operationally measurable terms, and provide the basis for performance measurement. OVIs act as a check on the viability of objectives and form the basis for the project monitoring system.

There are many different types of indicators, some more common than others, some better than others, some easier to collect than others, and some more widely recognized than others. For example, there are direct, indirect, process, and product indicators. In addition, there are qualitative and quantitative indictors. However, there are two types of objectively verifiable indicators: (1) quantitative indicators, which deal with things that can be counted and measured (for example, weekly church attendance), and (2) qualitative indicators, that are used to describe how the project functions and what it means to the people involved (stakeholders). Qualitative information is full of people's feelings so is better able to indicate how much of an affect a particular activity or program is having on the recipient group (Centre for International Development and Training 3-4.)

According to Wolverhampton University:

> Qualitative and Quantitative maxim for constructing an indicator generally works well. But its rigid application can result in performance and change that is difficult to quantify not being considered or given appropriate value. Change may be difficult to quantify or that the analysis of qualitative data may not be straightforward, are not reasons to sweep them under the carpet. Special effort and attention needs to be given to devising qualitative indicators. A balance of indicators is needed with some that focus on the quantitative and others on qualitative aspects.

## Outputs

Outputs are the results produced by undertaking a series of activities or what the project will have achieved by its completion date. The outcomes produced by the activities implemented over a five years period are: (1) to build relationships with other members (loving relationships strengthened); (2) to strengthen relationships with Christ (passionate spirituality strengthened); (3) to involve church members in mission (need-orientated evangelism increased); (4) to develop inspiring worship services; and (5) to cure sociological strangulation.

## STRATEGIC PLANNING FOR EVANGELISM

In structuring the church for evangelistic outreach, it is necessary to have a plan (possible a strategic plan) or vision for where you believe the Lord wants you and your church leadership team to be in the coming years (usually five to ten years).

In the example that follows, I have illustrated how this can be done by using the acronym of "Grace." The acronym represents the desired output and impact the leadership team and the congregation would like to see take place during the coming years. Each letter represents a specific output and impact in the churches strategic plans.

### GRACE

The flow chart, that follows, illustrates the strategic plan for the Reading District of Churches. Grace is a simple acronym that is easy to remember, yet complex in its overall objectives. Each letter represents an output which, it is hoped, will be accomplished by the programs implemented by the churches ministry departments and leadership.

The strategic plan output are as follows (see illustrations 3-6):

1. **G - Grow.** Numerical and Spiritual growth.
2. **R - Reach.** Reach internally and externally- evangelistic
3. **A - Assimilate** existing and new members into the mission and ministry of the church
4. **C - Connect and Commit**. Connecting members and visitors to the church and to ministry in accordance with their spiritual gifts).
5. **E - Exalt**. Inspiring worship services where God is the centre and Jesus is Lord. Worship services that creates an impact on the members and visitors.

96

In planning strategically for evangelism, it is advisable that the church devises short and long-term plans with clear aims and objectives. It should include targets (outcomes and outputs) for each evangelistic endeavours the church plans to undertake. This will help the church to better measure how    successful the program undertaken were.

In planning strategically,  each activity will generate a resource schedule, from which a cost will be generated. Each activity, in order to be effective, must be allocated its' required  resources (human, material, money, and method of accomplishing). These resources will contribute towards the overall evangelistic budget as well as the total costs for the short-term or long-term evangelistic plans for the church. The budget will provide the church with a clear picture of finances necessary over a given period and thereby the income necessary to facilitate the plans (see sample section for an example of a resource schedule).

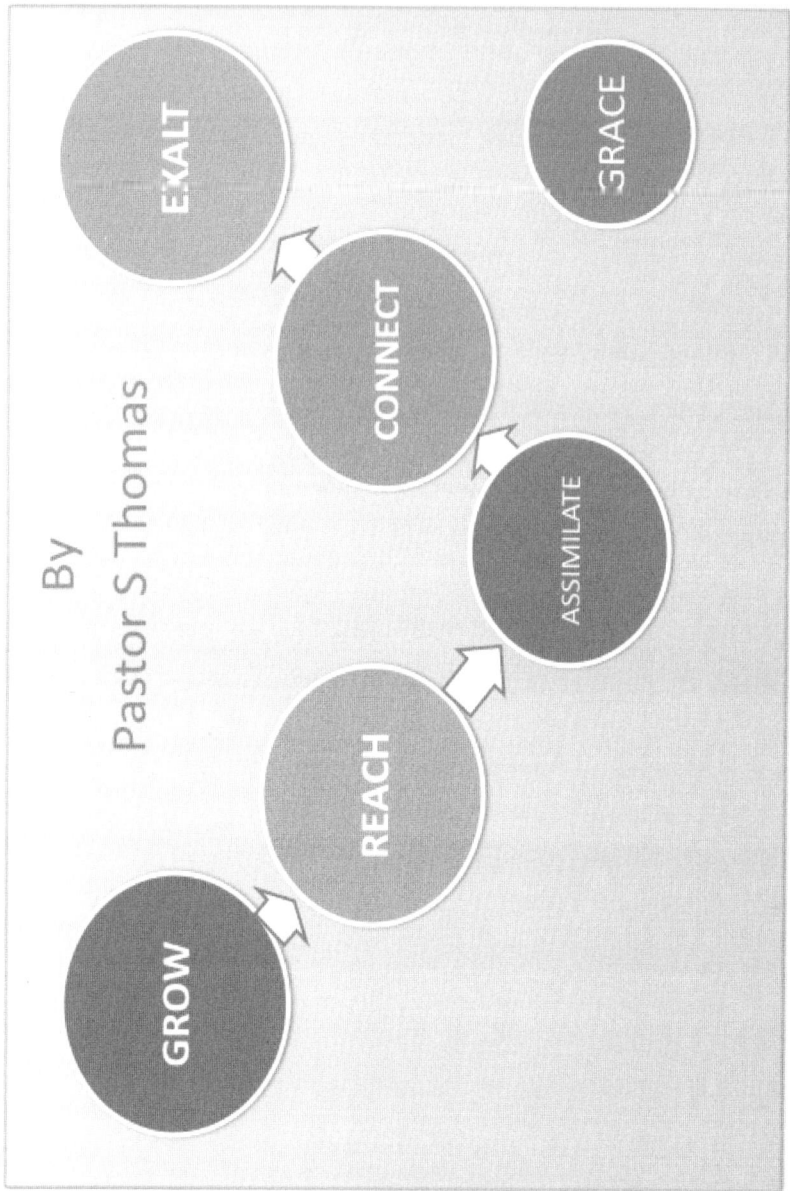

By
Pastor S Thomas

GROW

REACH

ASSIMILATE

CONNECT

EXALT

GRACE

Illustration No.3

# Grow....Nurturing God's people

- Bible Studies
- Daniel & Revelation Series
- Friendship & mentoring
- Practical ministry
- Teaching Series Sermons
- Week of Spiritual Emphasis

GRACE

# REACH...Helping/Leading someone to Christ or to understand their ministry (S.E.R.V.E)

- Bible Study
- Witnessing
- Teaching
- Friendship
- Mentoring
- Encouraging
- Evangelistic series
- Outreach through media etc

GRACE

**Above: GRACE** STRATEGIC PLAN: Grow; **Reach;** Assimilate; Connect; Exalt. Below: Examples of Implementing the GRACE strategic plan for effective evangelistic endeavours.

# GRACE SYSTEM OF STRATEGIC PLANNING
## Illustration No.5

Below: **E.Q.U.I.P** *(Empower members, Qualify them for Service, Understand their Needs, Instruct them, and Pray for them and the ministry God gave them)*

## CONNECT

- E.Q.U.I.P
- T.E.A.M

GRACE

Above: **T.E.A.M** *(Togetherness in ministry, Encourage them to Serve, Accountability, and Mentoring members)*

### ASSIMILATE

- Helping members and new believers Find their place and ministry within God's church
- Spiritual Gift tests and teachings
- Friendship evangelism
- Church Retreats, social events, And personal one-2-one visits
- Home2U ministry: inviting new
- Believers into your home for
- Sabbath lunch, Easter and seasonal Holidays.
- B-apart-of-me ministry

GRACE

# EXALT

Worship that is both evangelistic and Seeker sensitive

Worship that is expressive and creates an IMPACT

I – Inspirational

M - Motivational

P- Praise (Praising God in songs and testimonies and what we do)

A - Adoration (Adoring God in songs, poems, scripture and what we do)

C- Commit and Connect (Connecting people to God using the spoken word)

T- Trust (leave people trusting more in God and knowing that there is nothing to fear for the future except we forget how God has led us in the past)

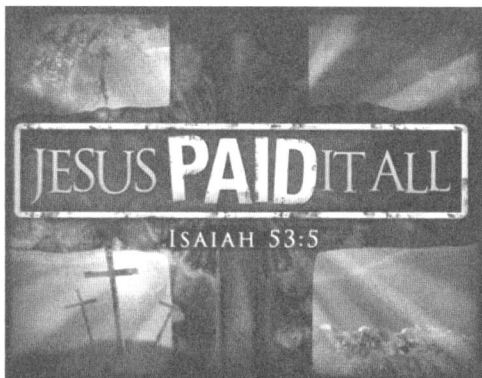

JESUS **PAID** IT ALL

ISAIAH 53:5

GRACE

*Worship that exalt:* *All heaven was given to us in Christ Jesus. . . . O honor Jesus by giving to Him the heart's best and holiest services! He has given His life for you. Who is He that hath done this? The only begotten Son of God, He that was One with the Father before the world was. If there was much more praising the Lord, and far less doleful recitation of discouragements, many more victories would be achieved. Let praise and thanksgiving be expressed in song. When tempted, instead of giving utterance to our feelings, let us by faith lift up a song of thanksgiving to God. Song is a weapon that we can always use against discouragement. As we thus open the heart to the sunlight of the Saviour's presence, we shall have health and His blessing. Lift up your banner, lift it up higher. Never, never let it trail in the dust of the earth. Exalt Jesus. Lift Him up, the Man of Calvary, higher and still higher. (White, Ministry of Healing, 1905).*

*Evangelism*

# Planning to Outreach Strategically

PLANNING

The central mission of the Seventh-day Adventist Church is to fulfil the gospel commission, "Therefore go and make disciples of all nations, baptizing them in the name of the Father and of the Son and of the Holy Spirit" (Matthew 28:19).

When properly understood, this should motivate us to do more than focus on quantity (number of baptisms). Included in our assignment is the call to love as Jesus loved; to be the "salt of the earth," and the "light" of our communities.

In His wisdom, God did not prescribe a required method for us to follow. There are literally hundreds and thousands of approaches that can be taken to "make disciples" and share God's love. God invites us to bring our unique talents and gifts to the table and dedicate them to this cause.

**Methods for Outreach Evangelism may include some of the following:**

1. Public meetings
2. Community work projects
3. Tutoring
4. Video lending library
5. Food bank
6. Personal Bible studies
7. Web evangelism
8. Church planting
9. Satellite seminars
10. Radio broadcasts
11. Television programs
12. Music ministry
13. Vacation Bible School

102

## OUTREACH COORDINATOR ( A Lay Evangelist)

The lay evangelist (Outreach person) dates to the time when Jesus sent out the seventy to minister in areas that He and the disciples would be unable to reach during His brief ministry (Luke 10:1-17). Just as these lay evangelists went out preaching the gospel of Jesus at His first coming, you are called to go and preach the gospel of His second coming. In the modern setting the lay evangelist reaches areas where the pastor or conference evangelist may never have the opportunity or budget to set foot. As a volunteer you can establish a work there.

The church serves the Lord in praise, serves one another in love, and serves the world in humility. "For we are his workmanship, created in Christ Jesus for good works, which God prepared beforehand, that we should walk in them" (Ephesians 2:10).

Jesus, in His last words before ascending to Heaven, gave the commission to "Go ye therefore, and teach all nations . . ." (Matthew 28:19): For the lay evangelist the target audience is the world, beginning at the doorstep of his or her home.

**Some of the duties:**

The work of the lay evangelist is varied, but some of the specific functions include the following:

1.  **Hold public evangelistic meetings.** Meetings could be in your town or in a nearby town where no formal Seventh-day Adventist work has been started. You could do all the preaching yourself, or organize a team to share the preaching duties. Don't overlook the possibilities of holding meetings for individuals in retirement centres, or for structuring your out-

reach to a specific ethnic group in your community. A series of meetings for the hearing impaired or other handicapped individuals who have special needs (that are often overlooked by regular outreach events) could be very rewarding.

2. **Conduct or Assist in conducting Daniel and Revelation seminars.** This form of public evangelism has been particularly effective in recent years with church members leading out. There is also material available to hold Daniel seminars which open up even more Bible prophecy to your hearers.

3. **Assist the pastor.** The lay evangelist can assist the pastor in evangelistic meetings or by preaching. Especially in a district with more than one church, the pastor needs the help of a lay minister to fill speaking appointments for Sabbath worship services and mid-week meetings from time to time. The pastor may also seek your assistance for visiting individuals who have shown an interest in learning more about Adventists.

4. **Organize neighbourhood outreach.** In cooperation with your church ministries leader, help plan outreach activities for your community, especially when laying the groundwork for evangelistic meetings with entry events, such as stop-smoking seminars, cooking and nutrition classes, etc.

5. **Recruit volunteers.** You will have the opportunity in your projects to minister to others in your church family by giving them the opportunity to become involved in active witnessing. Build a network of persons around you who also have a burden for soul-winning. Help train them for outreach ministry and encourage them to stay actively involved in witnessing.

6. **Small group evangelism.** Once called "cottage meetings," this form of outreach provides opportunities to

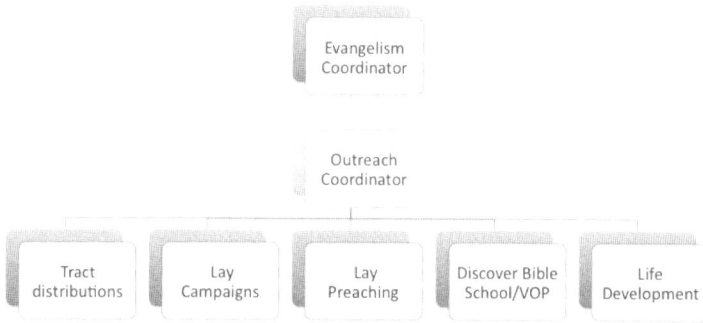

**Illustration No: 7** *Above: Proposed areas of responsibilities for Outreach coordinator -Reporting to Evangelism coordinator*

teach the gospel to two, three or a dozen individuals in a less formal situation. You may find this a good way to begin. An Evangelist is someone who has a burden to share the gospel in personal and public ways (depending upon their setting, personality and resources). Paul says Evangelism is a gift that God bestows on some of His followers. Usually a Lay Evangelist is someone who has another profession or livelihood, but their passion is to share the gospel. Typically, Lay Evangelist have not received training from a college or seminary. Often they are mentored by a pastor or friend who recognizes their gift.

**Evangelism methods employed include:**
1. Giving Bible Studies
2. Conducting community surveys
3. Personal visitation
4. Selling books and magazines
5. Public presentations (sermons)

## EVANGELISM DEPT AND NEW INREACH COORDINATOR

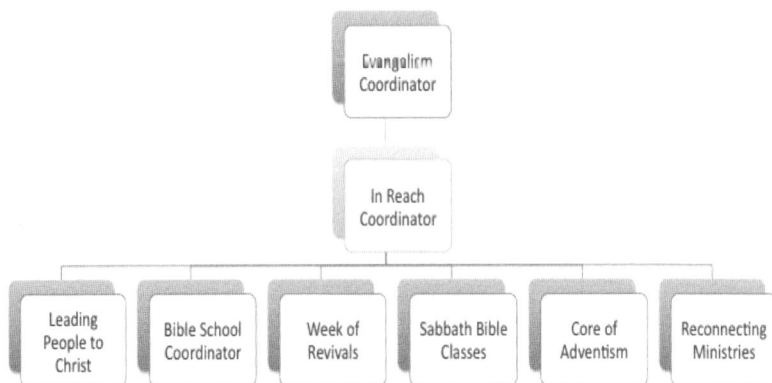

```
┌──────────────┐
│ Evangelism   │
│ Coordinator  │
└──────────────┘
        │
┌──────────────┐
│ In Reach     │
│ Coordinator  │
└──────────────┘
```

| Leading People to Christ | Bible School Coordinator | Week of Revivals | Sabbath Bible Classes | Core of Adventism | Reconnecting Ministries |

### INREACH COORDINATING MINISTRY
### (BIBLE SCHOOL AND NURTURING PERSON)

The last words of Christ before His departure from this world to those whom He had trained to carry on His work are of utmost importance to the church today. Notice His exact words: "But ye shall receive power, after that the Holy Ghost is come upon you; and ye shall be witnesses unto me both in Jerusalem, and in all Judea, and in Samaria, and unto the uttermost part of the earth" (Acts 1:8 KJV). This command was given not only to all those who heard Him speak, but also to all who would accept Him in the ages to come. They were to make known to the world the story of the Father's love and salvation.

Revival and church renewal take place when members use their Bibles to witness for Christ. Ellen White has written of "a great reformatory movement among God's people . . . Hundreds and thousands were . . . Visiting families, and opening before them the Word of God. Hearts were convicted by the power of the Holy Spirit, and a spirit of genuine conversion was manifest. On every side doors were thrown open to the proclamation of the truth. The world seemed to **be lightened with the heavenly** influence. Great blessings were received by the true and humble people of God" (Ellen G. White, Testimonies for the Church, Vol. 9, page 126).

**Some of the duties:**

The work to which a person is called when he or she becomes an Inreach coordinating minister can best be described as follows:

1. **Bible studies**. Most of the time that the Inreach coordinating ministry leader has available will be used to conduct personal Bible studies with individuals and families who have expressed an interest in studying the Word of God. Each study will take one or two hours a week. A regular routine of appointments is important in order to build relationships and help people grow in discipleship.

2. **Inquirers class.** Assist with the pastor's Bible class and bring their students to this class as they begin to attend church. (Sometimes the special Sabbath School class for prospective members is called the discovery class or visitor's class. It is often led by an elder or a lay Bible worker because the pastor has two or more congregations to work with each Sabbath and cannot attend Sabbath School).

3. **Missing member visits**. From time to time the pastor may assign the names of former or missing members to visit. This will give you contact with people with whom you will be able to study after you gain their friendship and confidence.

4. **An undershepherd.** The Inreach coordinating ministry leader will help the pastor seek and find the lost. He or she provides the pastoral caring and attention which the

pastor will not have the time to give to each prospective member. Often people turn to Christ and begin to think of joining a church at times of crisis in their lives. This means that the Inreach coordinating ministry leader must help to meet their emotional, economic and social needs as well as their spiritual needs and religious questions. Much time may be spent just listening. Time will also be invested in helping prospective members to make friends among church members, attend classes that are important to their growth, such as stop-smoking programs or family life seminars, and make use of the aid provided by Adventist Community Services and other social services.

5. **Finding prospects.** An Inreach Coordinating Ministry leader is constantly on the alert for people who may be ready to enter into Bible study. He or she will be sensitive to possibilities among friends, relatives, work associates, visitors at church, newcomers in the community, participants in outreach seminars and those who respond to Adventist media ministries and awareness activities. And he or she will learn to invite prospects to begin studies.

## Seminar Coordinator

God asks the church to be a community of people sharing a common purpose and fellowship, continually growing in faith and in the knowledge of the Son of God. Paul describes the church as "his body, the fullness of him who filleth every thing in every way" (Ephesians 1:22).

God supplies each person in the church with the resources for ministry—scripture, spiritual power, God's character, and spiritual gifts. A seminar coordinator is equipped for his or her ministry by the gifts received from the Holy Spirit. These spiritual gifts are special abilities given by the Holy Spirit to make their ministry effective and build up the body of Christ.

### Duties of the Seminar Coordinator

The ministry of the seminar coordinator includes the following duties:

**1. Planning.** You will work with the various Ministries, including Evangelism, Family, Pastoral and Youth Ministries, to develop an overall plan for seminars over the next year or two. This plan must be based on the identified needs in the congregation and the community, and a sequence of seminars moving from health education to family life, then Bible evangelism.

**2. Teamwork**. Involve a group of people with you in the planning stage. As you begin to think about the needs of your church and community, identify those church members who will be most productive in your seminar team. Rely on practical thinkers, good workers, people with ideas and imagination, and people who are good motivators and organizers. In the group you will need some who have excellent relational skills and can work one-on-one with the non-members who attend the seminars, develop friendships and invite them to church or into Bible studies.

**3. Program management**. Many details must be cared for by the seminar team such as arrangements for a location, obtaining materials and supplies, handling registration, obtaining and setting up equipment and the audio-visuals, and providing for greeters and other amenities at the seminar itself. Registration is a key part of the program because how it is handled and the materials handed out will give first impressions as to the value and warmth of the program. Child care is an important service if you wish to invite young married couples or single parents. It is vital that this all be smooth and friendly.

PLANNING

**4. Publicity.** A marketing approach must be developed for each seminar based on what audience group is targeted and their needs. You must arrange for advertising to be prepared and distributed well in advance, so that people can plan on attending and pre-register by phone. Advertising can be purchased through television and radio stations and newspapers. Posters, bus cards, and other forms of outdoor advertising may also be available. Direct mail is the most cost effective type of advertising. It will be your duty to obtain from the church interest coordinator (or prospect care coordinator) the prospect list, or help get the list started. This will be the key to advertising success. Mass mailings can also be arranged. And you are responsible for obtaining as much free publicity as possible through the news media and by encouraging church members to use word-of-mouth and distribute handbills among their friends, neighbours, relatives and work associates.

**5. Prayer support.** You will want to organize a network of "prayer warriors" to support the seminar through their intercessory prayer and especially to pray for those non-members in attendance. This may be done in groups or individually.

**6. Friendship evangelism.** A major purpose of seminar outreach is to establish friendships with non-members who attend. Small group discussion needs to be built into the program and church members used as the group leaders to give opportunity for acquaintances to be made. Feedback sheets used throughout the seminar build communication with individuals, and allow you to ask for specific decisions such as "Would you like for one of our staff to visit with you personally about the issues raised in the seminar?" As soon as the seminar is over, the prospect list must be updated and subscriptions to appropriate missionary magazines arranged for all who attended.

# Reviving and Organizing
# The Church for Service

Excerpts from Ellen G. White, Evangelism.
Reviving Church Members

The Lord does not now work to bring many souls into the truth, because of the church members who have never been converted, and those who were once converted but who have backslidden.

### First Train Church Members

In labouring where there are already some in the faith, the minister should at first seek not so much to convert unbelievers, as to train the church members for acceptable co-operation. Let him/her labour for them individually, endeavouring to arouse them to seek for a deeper experience themselves, and to work for others. When they are prepared to sustain the minister by their prayers and labours, greater success will attend his efforts.

### Clearing the King's Highway

When a special effort to win souls is put forth by labourers of experience in a community where our own people live, there rests upon every believer in that field a most solemn obligation to do all in his/her power to clear the King's highway, by putting away every sin that would hinder him/her from co-operating with God and with his/her brethren.

### An Example to New Converts

Older members should be an example to those who have recently join the church. Those who have been long in the truth are not to hurt the new converts by living irreligious lives. They should lay aside all murmuring and do thorough work in their own hearts. Break up the fallow ground of their hearts and seek to know what they can do to advance the work. Awake, awake, and give to the unconverted evidence that they believe the truth of heavenly origin. Unless they do awake, the world will not believe that they practice the truth that they profess to hold.

## The Church Members to Help

The Lord requires that far greater personal effort shall be put forth by the members of our churches. Souls have been neglected, towns and villages and cities have not heard the truth for this time, because wise missionary efforts have not been made.... Our ordained ministers must do what they can, but it must not be expected that one man can do the work of all. The Master has appointed unto every man his work. There are visits to be made, there is praying to be done, there is sympathy to be imparted; and the piety-the heart and hand-of the whole church is to be employed if the work is to be accomplished. They can sit down with their friends, and in a pleasant, social way, talk of the precious Bible faith.

## Ministers Enlist Churches in Evangelism

Sometimes ministers do too much; they seek to embrace the whole work in their arms. It absorbs and dwarfs them; yet they continue to grasp it all. They seem to think that they alone are to work in the cause of God, while the members of the church stand idle. This is not God's order at all.

## The Fields in Your Neighbourhood Are Ripe

The truth will triumph gloriously. Let the churches begin to do the work that the Lord has given them-- the work of opening the Scriptures to those who are in darkness. My brethren and sisters, there are souls in your neighbourhood who, if they were judiciously laboured for, would be converted. Efforts must be made for those who do not understand the Word. Let those who profess to believe the truth become partakers of the divine nature, and then they will see that the fields are ripe for the work that all can do whose souls are prepared by living the Word.

## Distributing Literature From Door to Door

Members should be prepared to walk from house to house, carrying the truth to the people. Sometimes they will find it trying to do this kind of work; but if they go forth in faith, the Lord will go before you, and will let His light shine upon their pathway. Entering the homes of their neighbours to sell or to give away our literature, and in humility to teach them the truth, they will be accompanied by the light of heaven, which will abide in these homes.

## Organizing Into Working Bands

In our churches let companies be formed for service. In the Lord's work there are to be no idlers. Let different ones unite in labour as fishers of men. Let them seek to gather souls from the corruption of the world into the saving purity of Christ's love. The formation of small companies as a basis of Christian effort is a plan that has been presented before me by One who cannot err. If there is a large number in the church, let the members be formed into small companies, to work not only for the church members but for unbelievers also.

# EFFECTIVE CHURCH PLANTING AND EVANGELISM

# 7

## EFFECTIVE CHURCH PLANTING AND EVANGELISM

### Planting New Churches

According to the monthly Missiological Reflections (MMRS), prepared by Dr. Gailyn Van Rheenen, Director of Mission Alive,

The theological and strategic foundations upon which churches are planted greatly affect their ability to grow and mature. Paul encourages the church planter to "be careful how he builds." Sooner or later the builder's work will be tested with fire. Those who build with incombustible materials (gold, silver, and costly stones) will receive a reward, but those who build with combustible materials (wood, hay, and straw) will experience loss (1 Cor. 3:10-15).

### Definition of Church Planting

Church planting is a process that results in a new Christian church being established. It should be distinguished from church development, where a new service, new worship centre or fresh expression is created that is integrated into an already established congregation. For a church to be planted, it must eventually have a separate life of its own and be able to function without its parent body, even if it continues to stay in relationship denominationally or through being part of a network.

Church planting may be defined as initiating reproductive fellowships who reflect the kingdom of God in the world. A number of characteristics of church planting are reflected in this definition.

First, church planting is aimed at the creation of fellowships. The church is the family of God, the body of Christ (Eph. 1:23), a people "belonging to God" (1 Pet. 2:9). These biblical metaphors indicate that the church must become a cohesive body reflecting the qualities of God in an alien world (vv. 11-12). Evangelistic methodologies should not scatter contacts who cannot be molded into bodies of believers; they must focus evangelism in one area for the purpose of creating a community of God. Converts must not be treated merely as individuals but incorporated in the body of Christ. Matayo Langat, a Kipsigis evangelist of Kenya, used a farming metaphor to explain why new Christians must work together to become part of a functioning fellowship:

> In Africa one person cannot cultivate with oxen by himself. There must be people in the field to guide the oxen on each side as well as one who holds the plow. Likewise, one cannot be the church by himself. He must call others who are in Christ to work together with him. (Translation from Kipsigis Sermon, 1976)

Donald McGavran concurs: "Would-be disciples must be joyfully built into his body-they must not wander alone in the wilderness" (1990, 7). Too frequently a few new Christians are left to fend for themselves after a short campaign. New converts are led to the Lord and then left before a fellowship of believers has come into existence. These few Christians will likely fall away from God because they have not been incorporated into a fellowship which can mold and guide them in their spiritual journey.

Second, effective church planting focuses on cultivating reproductive fellowships. Many times churches are established without expecting the new converts to teach others.

They are like seedless grapes, delightful to taste but without reproductive power, or the fig tree which Jesus withered because it did not bear fruit (Matt. 21:18-19).

Professor Wendell Broom has graphically described such churches as terminal (Broom 1976, 88-89). Terminal churches may have spiritual vitality but can reproduce only arithmetically (2, 4, 6, 8, 10, 12, 14, 16, 18, etc.). Church planters are teaching others but not training their converts to become reproductive; they are initiating churches but not preparing leaders of these churches to plant other churches.

Ten church planters can each plant one church each year. If the churches they plant have terminal life, after ten years their field will have 100 churches. If the planter die or return home, the number of churches remains static, for they do not plant other churches. The same ten planters, by planting churches that have germinal life, will in ten years have 5,110 churches in their field. If the planter die or return home, the churches will continue to multiply, because they have germinal life. (Broom 1976, 88)

The author of Hebrews described terminal churches when he wrote, "Though by this time you ought to be teachers, you need someone to teach you the elementary truths of God's word all over again. You need milk, not solid food!" (Heb. 5:12).

Germinal churches grow geometrically (2, 4, 8, 16, 32, 64, 128, 256, 512, etc.). They reproduce like rabbits in Australia, bananas in Bermuda, and papayas in fertile areas of tropical Africa. They are like starfish which multiply when cut into pieces. It is within the nature of each part to reproduce. Geometric church growth can be illustrated by strawberry plants or Bermuda grass, which send out runners in every direction; these runners develop their own root systems and send out still new runners until the field is covered. The roots each represent a new church or cell group planted in a new town or new area of the city. Once the Christian community develops sufficient roots it is able to plant still other fellowships. Paul urged Timothy to encourage his converts to become germinal: "The things you have heard me say in the presence of many witnesses (*germination 1*) entrust to reliable men (*germination 2*) who will also be qualified to teach others (*germination 3*)" (2 Tim. 2:2).

Greg Newton describes such germinal growth among the Sukuma of Tanzania. The first churches established among the Sukuma were missionary plants. The missionaries planned where they would preach and did all the teaching. The next six churches were co-plants. Sukuma Christians worked with missionaries in selecting the locations for establishing new churches, went with them each week to the meetings, and did some of the teaching, depending on their level of maturity. In March 1994, after three years of work among the Sukuma, two independent plantings occurred. The location of the plantings, plans for the evangelistic meetings, and the teaching in the area were all done without missionary participation (Newton 1994, 1). Germinal church growth had begun!

Third, church planting is more than the mere creation of fellowships. These fellowships must have accepted God as their sovereign and struggle to reflect his nature. Thus church planting is the developing of reproductive fellowships which reflect the kingdom of God in the world. The term fellowship expresses the horizontal relationships between Christians within the body; the phrase which reflect the kingdom of God in the world expresses the vertical relationship between God and the fellowship over which he reigns. This distinction is vital because a church fellowship can divorce itself from the divine and become largely a social fraternity, much like the local Kiwanis or Rotary club. This type of fellowship has no divine impetus to germinate.

Fourth, this definition assumes that nurturing must follow the initial planting of the church. Bodies of believers are not superficially planted and then left but cared for until they "re-

PLANTING

119

flect the kingdom of God in the world." The term initiating implies that something must follow the planting of the church.

## Motivation for Growth

Certain Christian beliefs provide special impetus to germinal growth. Anticipation of and preparation for the second coming of Christ is one such belief. When Christians perceive of themselves as standing between the first and second comings of Christ, they are motivated to teach those around them to prepare for his return. The reality that this world is temporary- that their real identity is in heaven-helps disciples of Christ to understand their place in the world and propels them to speak of eternal realities. The understanding that God is active and is convicting the world of sin through the Holy Spirit (John 16:7-11) is another germinal belief. Christians who believe in God's mighty acts will be ready when the Holy Spirit touches them to teach a Cornelius or an Ethiopian. Their lives are tuned in to God's reality rather than secular "realities" which deny the active working of God. Greg Newton reflects upon the great church growth among the Sukuma with this comment: "We praise God for the Spirit which is moving to inspire Christians to evangelize" (Newton 1994, 1). Belief in the temporary nature of this world and the working of the Holy Spirit are thus two beliefs foundational to germinal growth.

### Guidelines for Effective Planting of New Churches

Specifics of church planting vary from context to context. However, four general guidelines are fundamental in every context.

**First, church planters must look at their work as a spiritual activity.** They must pray and fast both for the city or ethnic group in which God has placed them and for God's empowerment for the task of evangelizing. They must realize that the people of this particular area have not previously become followers of God because they are still under the dominion of Satan. Christ, however, has come "to destroy the devil's work" (1 John 3:8). Church planters, therefore, must *pray for wisdom and empowerment from God realizing that evangelization is ultimately taking territory that once belonged to Satan and claiming it for the kingdom of God.* Prayer is an admission of God's role, an acknowledgement that only God in Jesus Christ can deliver the people from the grip of sin and clutches of the evil one. Evangelizing unbelievers and nurturing them to grow in Christ is not primarily a human endeavour but God's working through his people.

**Second, church planters must visualize what God's church should look like within their target culture and seek to implement this vision.** In every culture the church must reflect the presence of God because it is the distinctive people of God called by him through his mission and set aside for his mission. However, the forms of church vary from culture to culture. These forms include such items as language, worship, and decision-making. Should a Russian church speak English in worship services and be reliant upon American models of church? Should the songs reflect the rhythms and harmonies of Western music? Christian meanings must be communicated in indigenous forms. The people of the land should not perceive the church as a foreign religion but as a part of indigenous society. This does not mean that Christianity will be compromised or that syncretism with non-Christian religious elements will take place. It means that Christian be-

PLANTING

121

liefs will be communicated in terms acceptable and meaning-
ful to the culture in which the church is planted. Like a banana
plant in the Bahamas, the church thrives within the culture
because it allows God to use the resources of the culture rather than superficially borrowing cultural forms from a foreign
source. However, should there be a need to have services in
the language of the majority in attendance, then the church,
as a means of allowing the gospel to impact the majority lives,
should conduct the services in that language.

Despite the above, never should the church forget the mission of reaching all people, especially the community where
the church is located. This would allow the church to carry
out the Lord's commission.

**Third, church planters must learn to communicate**
God's eternal message within the plausibility structures of
the people in the culture. The thought that Christ has defeated
the principalities and powers (Col. 1:15) has little impact on
the seculars in your community, who have little understanding of spiritual powers. This concept of Christ, the triumphal
One who has defeated the spirits, however, is the metaphor
which stirs the heart of the animist and brings him to the
foot of the cross (Van Rheenen 1991, 141-42). Only in Christ
is there deliverance from the fear and control of the satanic
realm. Church-planting planters thus enter a new culture as
learners seeking to glean understandings concerning how to
communicate God's message and to initiate a church which
reflects the kingdom of God within this cultural context.

**Fourth, church planters must learn what web relation-
ships tie people of the culture together**. Kinship, although
more dominant in rural societies than in urban cultures, is the
dominant web relationship. In Africa, Asia, and Latin America,
the web counts tremendously. Every man has, knows and is
intimate with not merely brothers, sisters, and grandparents,
but also with cousins, uncles, aunts, great-uncles, sisters-in-
law, mothers-in-law ... And many others. Members of other

PLANTING

clans or families can become Christian and he remains un-moved; but let "one of us" become Christian and he is deeply stirred. (McGavran 1970, 321)

## Models of church planting

There are several models of church planting. The model of church plant will be determined by the leaders and is best chosen to fit the needs of the community in which the church will be started. The following are some of the models of church plant:
- Parachute drop
- Mother/daughter
- Partnership network
- House churches
- Multi-site church
- Restart
- Split

## Parachute drop

A church planter and their family move into a new location to start a church from scratch. The planter has very little connection with or existing support within the new area. The planter and their family are "pioneering" new territory. Where there is great risk, there is great reward, but this approach is not for the faint of heart and requires a person particularly gifted in personal evangelism. Advantages of this approach include flexibility, and the ability to reach otherwise unreached areas. The disadvantages might be the effort required to integrate with a new community, and possible lack of financial and personal support.

PLANTING

## Mother/daughter

An existing church or church planting organisation (mother) provides the initial leadership and resources (money and/or people) to get a new church (daughter) started. This includes the selection of the church planter. Often the church planter is selected from within the organisation and already agrees with the vision, values and beliefs of the sponsoring organisation, or has been employed with a view to planting. The existing relationship allows for a close working relationship between the "mother" and "daughter" churches. Although the new church is autonomous, the sponsoring organisation often has significant influence in the new church (including decision making during the prelaunch phase). Advantages often include increased financial resources and the ability to draw core team / launch team members from the sponsoring organisation.

## House churches

Small groups form and multiply via a network of people meeting in homes. In some cases, the individual cells are connected in a larger network that meets together periodically in a large group setting. This relational model focuses on personal growth, care and teaching through one-on-one and small group discipleship. Groups are birthed through multiplication, and, often die, only to resurface months or even years later. This model requires very little funding.

## Multi-site church

An existing church opens new locations. This is attractive to larger churches, which explains why Willow Creek Community Church has moved in this direction. Smaller churches have also successfully implemented the strategy. Motives range from reaching more non-Christian to making more room at an existing location. The evolving multi-site model is proving im-

**PLANTING**

portant in creating an entrepreneurial spirit of multiplication within existing churches. Where multi-site multiplication results in multiple leadership teams and replication of all aspects of church, then this method is a relevant form of church planting; (see Ichthus Christian Fellowship). Where the new expression is integrated into the current organisational unit, then no church plant has occurred, merely an extension work of an existing congregation.

## Restart

An existing struggling church decides to bury the old and plant a fresh new church. The restart may or may not be at a new location and may or may not be with the same leadership. The resources of many older stagnant churches are a good way to bring new life to the community being served.

## Split

This is not really a church planting method, but nonetheless is the agency through which many new churches occur. A split typically occurs when competing groups conclude there is less energy required to "split" or "divorce" than to resolve differences and reconcile. The underlying factors causing the split often develop over years. In many cases, the dysfunctional character traits of the old church carry forward to the new churches, but the passion on both sides of the argument can often lead to surprising growth. Not to be recommended as a strategy!

PLANTING

# PREPARING
# THE
# CHURCH

# 8

## PREPARING THE CHURCH

The Holy Spirit works in powerful ways when we seek His power and plead for souls through intercessory prayer. When the church fails to pray powerfully, God does not move powerfully.

Soul winning is first and foremost God's work. He wins souls—we do not. He transforms lives, converts hearts, and changes people. His power, poured out through us, makes the difference. Although He invites us to cooperate with Him and gives us the joy of participating in His work, He is the Master Soul winner.

Intercessory prayer puts us in touch with His strength and wisdom. It
prepares our hearts for Him to do something special through us. As we pray, God works in ways that He would not work if we did not pray. Our prayers are an acknowledgement of our dependence on Him.

In prayer, we acknowledge that we cannot but that He can. Ellen White states it succinctly, when she writes, "God will grant in answer to the prayer of faith that which He would not do if we did not thus ask" (GC 525)—and "Prayer and faith will do what no power on earth can accomplish" (MH 509).

In the great controversy between good and evil, God respects our freedom of choice. He will never manipulate the will. He will never force or coerce our choices. Before our unsaved loved ones ever turn to Him, He is working to influence their lives for the kingdom, but He will only go so far. They must ultimately choose for or against Christ. When we pray for souls,

PREPARING

127

God works more powerfully, because He respects our freedom of choice to seek Him on their behalf (see 1 John 5:16-21). Prayer does make a difference. Praying churches experience the miracle-working power of God.

### Practical Suggestions

1. Select prayer group leaders. Keep your groups fairly small (6–10 people).
2. Encourage your prayer groups to meet once a week at a time they choose, to pray for specific things regarding the upcoming evangelistic meetings.
3. Encourage your prayer groups to pray for:
   - Non–Adventist spouses and family members
   - Former Seventh-day Adventists
   - Contacts of church members
   - Media interests
   - All public advertising for the series
   - Pray for specific people by name:

     *"Oh, that one might plead with God for a man"* (Job 16:21).

     *"Why do not two or three meet together and plead with God for the salvation of some special one, then still another"* (7T 21, 22).

     *"Angels are waiting around the throne of God to instantly obey the command of Christ in answer to every prayer offered in living faith"* (2SM 371).

4. Launch your prayer ministry approximately four months before the evangelistic series begins.
5. Meet with your prayer band leaders every other week to encourage them and share updates on answered prayer and new prayer agenda request items.
6. Share answers to prayer with the congregation on Sabbath mornings to encourage them to participate in the ministry of intercession.
7. Continue your prayer ministry during the evangelistic series by inviting your "Prayer Warriors" to meet one-

PREPARING

half hour before the nightly evangelistic meetings to pray. Be sure to have all prayer groups attend the meetings and listen to the evangelistic sermons, praying quietly in the meetings for the outpouring of the Spirit.

## Acts 1:14 Praying for Empowerment

Evangelistic churches emphasise prayer, especially prayer for the lost. Church growth experts like Peter Wagner have stressed the necessity of prayer in evangelism and church growth. Correct methods are important, but they are no substitute for prayer. The power of the Holy Spirit must animate the principles and methods (John Mark Terry, Church Evangelism, 1997, 15).

Thom Rainer says that a dynamic church must first become "a house of prayer," and he devotes a whole chapter in his book, *Giant Awakenings,* to congregational prayer. Ken Hemphill writes that "the fuel for all growth is powerful prayer." Hemphill is not speaking of typical church prayers: We spend more time praying to keep dying saints who are prepared to die... than we do to keep sinners from hell fire.
Pray for Power

If the Holy Spirit left your church today, would anyone notice? Does anything happen in your congregation that is not clearly due to human efforts? Too few Christians and too few Christian churches are characterised by the anointing of the Holy Spirit. Many church members are like those whom Paul described as "having a form of godliness but denying its power" (2 Tim. 3:5). If they do not deny the power of the Holy Spirit with their lips, they deny it with their lives.

We have the best in materials, media, and methods, but we lack spiritual power. Christians of the apostolic era had none of our advantage; they didn't even have the New Testament. Still, they turned the Roman Empire upside down. What impact does your church have in your community?

PREPARING

We cannot evangelize without God's power. The first two chapters of Acts provide us with a case study of prayer and empowerment. In Acts 1:4-5 Jesus told his disciples: "Do not leave Jerusalem, but wait for the gift of my Father promised, which you have heard me speak about. For John baptized with water, but in a few days you will be baptized with the Holy Spirit." Then he commanded them: "But you will receive power when the Holy Spirit comes on you; and you will be my witnesses" (v.8). Notice that empowerment comes before witness.

The disciples did as Jesus instructed them; Jesus told them to wait in Jerusalem for empowerment. Acts 1:14 records their obedience: "They all joined together constantly in prayer, along with the women and Mary the mother of Jesus, and his brothers." The disciples prayed in the upper room for ten days, waiting for the Holy Spirit's anointing. According to Acts 2:2, when the day of Pentecost arrived, the disciples "were all together in one place." What were they doing? They were praying together, just as they had for the past ten days.

What did the disciples pray for? R. A. Pegram (Church Growth Through Intercessory Prayer, *Good News: September-October 1995:24)*, answers the question:

At Pentecost, I believe the disciples were praying not only for themselves, but also for the people of Jerusalem who had rejected Jesus. Many of those who had rejected Jesus were relatives, friends, acquaintances, and business associates. The disciples were interceding for Jerusalem with a oneness purpose. They wanted to see people come to believe in their resurrected Lord. When they Holy Spirit fell on those who were praying, I believe they were so filled with God's love that their prayers were set on fire for the people they knew."

The disciples prayed for both power and results, and God answered both their requests. The Holy Spirit came on the apostles like a rushing wind, and they bravely stood and boldly declared the gospel. What a remarkable transformation! Fifty days before, these same men had cowered in locked rooms because they were afraid. Now they stood and proclaimed the gospel to the same people who had frightened them before.

Not only were the apostles empowered; their prayer for lost souls were answered. When Peter finished preaching, he gave an invitation and three thousand people responded. Notice that the wonderful response followed ten days of intense prayer and empowerment by the Holy Spirit. This is no magic formula, but the implication are clear. If we spent more time in prayer, we would have more power in our evangelistic efforts.

One would think that the church in Jerusalem stopped evangelizing in order to nurture the three thousand people just baptized. Not so. Acts 2:42 tells us that the Christians continued to devote themselves to prayer. What were the results of this fervent prayer? According to verses 43-47, the apostles performed miracles; the Christians were unified; they shared their possessions with the poor; they continued to worship daily; they met together in homes for fellowship; they won the favour of the people in Jerusalem, and they saw people come to believe in Christ every day.

If you compare the situation in the Jerusalem church with that of many modern churches, what comes to mind? Many of our churches today are divided into warring camps. Thousands of churches baptize no one in a given year. Most communities find the church irrelevant. What makes the difference? The power of the Holy Spirit. In order to fulfil the Great Commission, the church must access the power of the Holy Spirit through prayer. We need Spirit-empowered preaching, witnessing, and ministry. As Jesus said, "Apart from me you can do nothing" (John 15:5).

PREPARING

131

---

PREPARING

# What Should We Do?

Pray for Guidance

Just before he ascended into heaven, Jesus told his disciples: "Stay in the city until you have been clothed with power from on high" (Luke 24:48). Why did Jesus say that? Jesus knew his disciples desperately needed the Spirit's empowerment. They would have gone into spiritual battle unarmed without it. Similarly, Jesus also knew that they needed guidance. How could they know where to go or what to do without the Spirit's guidance?

We may ask the same question of Jesus' modern disciples. How can we know where to go or what to do without guidance? How are almost unlimited needs and opportunities for ministry in every community-not to mention the overwhelming needs in the world. Obviously, a single congregation can't do everything. So, what do you do, and where should you do it? The Holy Spirit will answer those questions. If we pray for guidance and remain sensitive and alert to the Spirit's direction, the Spirit will direct us.

There are several examples of the Spirit's guidance in the Book of Acts. Acts 8 tells the story of Philip and the Ethiopian eunuch.

Pray for Results

The first Christians prayed powerfully. Much of our contemporary prayer is either pointless or selfish. Many congregational prayers are so general they are meaningless. Most of our private prayers are wish lists of things we want God to give us or do for us. Acts 2:24-30 reports a remarkable different prayer offered by the members of the Jerusalem congregation. They prayed that God would enable them to preach with boldness and perform miraculous signs in the name of Jesus. What happened when they prayed this way? "After they prayed, the place they were meeting was shaken. And they were all filled with the Holy Spirit and spoke the word of God boldly" (Acts 4:31). Notice the progression here: prayer, power, and finally proclamation. If we prayed as they prayed, we would be empowered as they were and we would preach as they preached.

### Teach Members to Pray

Many do not know how to pray. How do people learn to pray? By observation, instruction, and participation. Jesus' disciples saw him praying. Jesus often got up early in the morning and went to a solitary place in order to pray. We know that Jesus' example of prayer made a deep impression on the apostles, because they asked the church in Jerusalem to elect deacons so they would have more time to pray (Acts 6:4). Pastors and church leaders should model prayer for their people, not to be praised (Matt. 6:5-6), but in order to teach them. One's motive is the key factor here. We model prayer by praying and by the way we pray. When you pray, simply so that new believers can imitate you.

Believers also learn to pray by instruction. Jesus' disciples asked him, "Teach us to pray" (Luke 11:1). In response Jesus taught them the Lord's Prayer, or better, the "Model Prayer." You would do well to lead your people in a study of this prayer. The pastor should preach on prayer and lead a study group on prayer. The attendance may not be overwhelming, but it is better to disciple a few than none at all.

### Develop a Prayer Ministry

There are many ways to develop a prayer ministry. The important thing is to do it. In most churches prayer is an activity, but not an intentional ministry. Here, we are seeking a fine balance. Some things can be organized to death, so that

**PREPARING**

nothing spontaneous happens. Organizing your prayer ministry will ensure that the church prays consistently and comprehensively. It will also pay dividends in evangelism. Some of the ministry activities that could be included in your prayer ministry are listed:

- Prayer Partners
- Prayer Chains
- Prayer Groups
- Special Days of Prayer
- Host Prayer Seminars
- Set Up A Prayer Room
- Host Prayer Retreats
- Host Twenty-four Hour Prayer Ministries
- Host Prayer Hot lines
- Do A Prayer Walk with Prayer Walkers

According to Russell Burrill, "everything can be in readiness for the meetings to begin—handbills mailed, sermons prepared, organization set up, etc.—Yet the meeting can still prove to be a failure. This can happen if the church members are not sufficiently equipped for the meetings. The preparation of members is a key to success in evangelism." (Russell Burrill, 2007). Burrill suggests that "if the church is not sowing ahead of time, there will be no harvest when the meetings take place." The exception to this is if the body of Christ, the Church, is healthy and functioning according to its mandate, where every member is a minister and where members are actively engaged in some form of evangelism.

If this is so, then, according to Burrill, "the meetings can happen at anytime, and there will always be people who can be reached." However, seeing that most churches are far from the ideal of always being in a "ready" status, the following were suggested by Burrill as suitable for preparing the church for evangelistic meetings:

1. Prayer Strategy
2. Prayer, Consecration, and Communion Service

3. Friendship Evangelism
4. Need-Oriented Seminars
5. Bible Studies
6. Small Groups Ministry

In addition, one could add

7. Week of Spiritual Emphasis/Revivals, and
8. Daniel and Revelation Seminars
9. LIFEdevelopment

For further information, please refer to Russell Burrill's Step-by-step guide to public evangelism. The pages that follows are excerpts from this guide, for the purpose of giving you a "quick-start" to the preparation process for evangelistic meetings. However, it is highly recommended that you acquire the guide as it provides detailed information on Public Evangelism (Russell Burrill, *Reaping the Harvest*, 2007).

**PREPARING**

### Prayer Strategy

Ellen White wrote in
> The up building of the kingdom of God is retarded or urged forward according to the unfaithfulness or fidelity of human agencies. The work is hindered by the failure of the human to cooperate with the divine. Men may pray, "Thy kingdom come. Thy will be done in earth, as it is in heaven"; but if they fail of acting out this prayer in their lives, their petitions will be fruitless (White, *Christian Services*).

She further adds, "All heaven is looking upon the inhabitants of the earth. The angels and the God of heaven are looking upon those who claim to be Christians, and weighing their devotional exercises."

According to Burrill, "the most important thing you can do in preparation for the meetings is to get the church members praying for them." This, he says, "will do more than anything else to get people on board. It is hard to be unsupportive of the meetings while praying regularly for their success."

His program commences at least six to eight months before the start of the meetings, and involve:

1. **Six to eight months before the meeting:** The Evangelist begins a special prayer warrior ministry
2. **Six to eight months before the opening night**: Preach a sermon on the power of the Holy Spirit and the centrality of prayer in preparation for the meetings. Commitment slips are distributed to the members so they can sign up to be a prayer warrior on behalf of the meetings

**3. There are three levels of prayer warriors**

1. *Level 1 Prayer Warrior:* Pray daily for the evangelistic meetings as part of their regular devotional life. In addition, the person agrees to meet with the other prayer warriors after church each Sabbath to pray for the outpouring of the Spirit in the meetings. They also agree to meet for one hour each month in order to pray for the meetings and the people in the community. They are expected to attend the special prayer, communion, and consecration service the week before the meetings.
2. *Level 2 Prayer Warriors* is an advanced level which includes prayer walks, and
3. *Level 3 Prayer Warriors the Superior level*, which includes the role of knocking on the doors of the people living in the community. They inform the residents that they are from the Adventist Church and have been praying for the people in the community—and wonder if there are any special prayer requests that they could pray for?

After praying for the requests for a couple of weeks, the member returns to the home to inquire how things are going in response to their prayers and to ask if there are other requests. Over a number of weeks and months the Prayer Warrior continues to return to the homes and ultimately will end up developing a relationship with those who have responded to prayer requests. As they see spiritual interest developing, they invite their new friends to attend the prayer time and join in praying for the neighbourhood. Those who respond make excellent contacts to invite to the meetings when the time comes.

In addition, the Prayer Warriors meet during the evangelistic meetings to pray for the evangelist and for the Spirit of God to win out as people struggle with the truths of God's word.

**Prayer, Consecration, and Communion Service**

This is a four-hour service conducted on the Sabbath before the meetings begin. The main reason for four hours is to allow time for the Holy Spirit to work on people's hearts. The program is scheduled as follows:

### Session 1 (the first hour)

1. **Song Service** (10 minutes)
2. **Prayer Session involving seven areas members should pray for:**
   - Pray for the yourself to fully confess your sins in order to make yourself available for the Holy Spirit
   - Pray for the church and for the majority of the members to be fully involved in reaching the lost
     - Pray for the evangelistic team as they present the message each night

- Pray for those who attend the meetings that they will be impressed by the Spirit with the truths that they hear
- Pray for the nightly meetings that the devil will not be able to come through and disrupt the meetings
- Pray for the former members to come and take their stand for Jesus once more
- Pray for visitors to make the decision to follow Jesus

### Session 2 (the 2nd hour)

1. **Revival and Reformation:** Readings from Ellen White along with explanations. Emphasis on claiming the promises of God for people's salvation.

### Session 3 (the 3rd hour)

1. **Sacrificial Prayer**—One hour of Prayer for Power
   - Praise Prayer (15 minutes)
   - Public confession—not specific personal sins (15 minutes)
   - Praying for people who need to find Jesus (15 minutes)
   - Time for healing—inviting people who need prayer for healing to come forward, while the rest gather in a circle around them (15 minutes)

### Session 4 (the final hour)

5. **The Lord's Supper**
   1. Agape feast communion with fruits, nuts and grains
   2. Use a table layout similar to a cross
   3. Foot-washing is done without talking, but re-

flecting on the word of God and singing songs. Here a schedule program is necessary to keep it simple and flowing and spiritually based

4. Songs reflecting on the goodness of God can be played accompanied by visual images
5. Close up the meeting with a song of hope, such as "Blest Be the Tie that Binds."

### Friendship Evangelism

There are several programmes available for the church to conduct friendship evangelism training. They cover the same basic material. The main thing to note is that of writing out a plan. Valuable information may remain unused unless the evangelist encourages the members to put their plans on paper.

### Need Oriented Seminars

These programmes are targeted to the specific needs of the people in the community, for the purpose of building relationships with new people: For example:

1. Stop Smoking seminars
2. Vegetarian Cooking classes
3. Financial Management
4. Stress seminars
5. Drug-free seminars
6. Parenting seminars
7. Health Expo

### Bible Studies

This is one of the essential elements in preparation for the meetings. It is important to make certain that Bible studies are being given to all interested people. The friendship and need-oriented events should be producing people who are beginning to enquire about what Adventists believe. Bible studies can be arranged with these people.

PREPARING

## Week of Spiritual Emphasis/Revival

When churches are revived, it is because some individual seeks earnestly for the blessing of God. He hungers and thirsts after God, and asks in faith, and receives accordingly. He goes to work in earnest, feeling his great dependence upon the Lord, and souls are aroused to seek for a like blessing, and a season of refreshing falls on the hearts of men. The extensive work will not be neglected. The larger plans will be laid at the right time; but personal, individual effort and interest for your friends and neighbors, will accomplish much more than can be estimated. It is for the want of this kind of labor that souls for whom Christ died are perishing. (White, *Christian Services*)

One soul is of infinite value; for Calvary speaks its worth. One soul, won to the truth, will be instrumental in winning others, and there will be an ever-increasing result of blessing and salvation. Your work may accomplish more real good than the more extensive meetings, if they lack in personal effort. When both are combined, with the blessing of God, a more perfect and thorough work may be wrought; but if we can have but one part done, let it be the individual labor of opening the Scriptures in households, making personal appeals, and talking familiarly with the members of the family, not about things of little importance, but of the great themes of redemption. Let them see that your heart is burdened for the salvation of souls. (White, Review and Herald, March 13, 1888).

## LIFEdevelopment

LIFEdevelopment is a new, but long-term evangelistic strategy of the Seventh-day Adventist Church. Its purpose is to build bridges with people who may have no initial interest in organized religion.

Its primary focus is on encouraging friendships between church members and secular people and creating an atmosphere which allows unchurched people to discover for them-

**PREPARING**

selves, in their own time, what Christianity is all about. It is divided into phases. In its **first phase**, entitled "Get Connected." LIFEdevelopment concentrates on making personal friendships, building small friendship groups, encouraging holistic small groups, forming LIFEdevelopment centres, and networking all of these together. The **second and third phases** uses a series of television programmes entitled "Evidence," and "Mind the Gap," presented by Dwight Nelson, which focuses on life issues such as stress, forgiveness, and hope. Later phases include training and "discipling."

# Discipling[1]

*Then Jesus approached and said to them, "All power in heaven and on earth has been given to me. Go, therefore, and make disciples of all nations, baptizing them in the name of the Father, and of the Son, and of the holy Spirit, teaching them to observe all that I have commanded you. And behold, I am with you always, until the end of the age."*

*Matthew 28:18-20 (New American Bible)*

---

1 "**Reprinted by permission**. Rediscovering Pastoral Ministry: Shaping Contemporary Ministry with Biblical Mandates, by John MacArthur and Master's College Faculty, 1995, published Thomas Nelson Inc. Nashville, Tennesse. All rights reserved."

# 9

## DISCIPLING

God has called pastors to the indispensable task of discipleship. Both the Old and New Testaments mark out discipleship as a requisite part of ministry—not an option. Jesus, the greatest disciple-maker, utilized four reproducible principles in His ministry, which remain equally relevant today. They are prayerful meditation, careful selection, purposeful association, and powerful proclamation. The Scripture never refers to a non discipling shepherd; it commends only reproducing pastors.

Biblical instruction about disciple-making dates as far back as Jethro's counsel to Moses to choose godly men to help him adjudicate the affairs of Israel. Jethro's own words are,

> Now listen to me: I shall give you counsel.... You shall select out of all the people able men who fear God, men of truth, those who hate dishonest gain; and you shall place these over them, as leaders of thousands, of hundreds, of fifties and of tens. And let them judge the people at all times; and let it be that every major dispute they will bring to you, but every minor dispute they themselves will judge. So it will be easier for you, and they will bear the burden with you. If you do this thing and God so commands you, then you will be able to endure, and all these people also will go to their place in peace (Exod. 18:19, 21–23).

PRACTICING

143

## The Mandate for Discipling

Discipling in the Old Testament

Moses learned well from his father-in-law and told the men of Israel in the wilderness, "How can I alone bear the load and burden of you and your strife? Choose wise and discerning and experienced men from your tribes, and I will appoint them as your heads" (Deut. 1:12–13). Also, what Moses commanded for the effective leadership in the daily affairs of Israel, he saw as the need also for future generations:

And these words, which I am commanding you today, shall be on your heart; and you shall teach them diligently to your sons and shall talk of them when you sit in your house and when you walk by the way and when you lie down and when you rise up. And you shall bind them as a sign on your hand and they shall be as frontals on your forehead. And you shall write them on the doorposts of your house and on your gates" (Deut. 6:6–9; cf. 11:18–21; 16:18–20).

Moses instituted a discipling process between fathers and sons (and even grandsons) that would ensure godly leadership in the home and society for God's people, both then and in the future. Wherever a need exists to discern God's will in the affairs of men—in the world or home—the clearly prescribed principle is to develop leadership through making disciples.

As an example, Moses did not leave Israel without leadership. He discipled Joshua with the result that "the Lord exalted Joshua in the sight of all Israel; so that they revered him, just as they had revered Moses all the days of his life" (Josh. 4:14; cf. Exod. 24:13; 33:11; Num. 11:28). Moses handed down an administrative principle: Reproduce yourself in others so that the leadership of God's people will continue throughout your generations.

Through the rest of the Old Testament, the same principle was very obvious in the training relationship between Elisha and Elijah (1 Kings 19:19–21; 2 Kings 2:3; 3:11) and in that between Baruch and Jeremiah (Jer. 36:26; 43:3). Samuel seemed to have a group of prophets under his oversight too (1 Sam. 10:5–10; 19:20–24).

One suggestion has been that these "individual master-disciple relationships within the leadership of the nation enabled the leadership function to be passed from one leader to the next until God had accomplished his purposes through them to meet the need of his people." (Michael Wilkins, 1992). The same author has summarized the Old Testament concept of discipleship as follows:

Master-disciple relationships behind the perpetuation and dissemination of the wisdom tradition would be found in informal father-son relationships, in training of elders for making judicial decisions in the city gate, in the wisdom orientation of advisers in the court, and within certain groups who specialized in wisdom and were involved with the recording of wisdom sayings.

Discipling, whether called that or not, is the heartbeat of wise counsel in the Old Testament: "Iron sharpens iron, so one man sharpens another" (Prov. 27:17).

### Discipling in the New Testament

Following these examples from the Old Testament, pastors should keep endeavoring to build themselves into others. This is not just a worthwhile option; it is a mandate from the Word of God!

The mandate from Jesus. Jesus Christ Himself commanded that His disciples (and in turn all who follow in their lineage) make disciples of others. Matt. 28:18–20 records that nonnegotiable imperative:

PRACTICING

145

And Jesus came up and spoke to them, saying, "All authority has been given to Me in heaven and on earth. Go therefore and make disciples of all the nations, baptizing them in the name of the Father and the Son and the Holy Spirit, teaching them to observe all that I commanded you; and lo, I am with you always, even to the end of the age."

Because of the context, it is possible to say that Christians and disciple-makers are synonymous terms. If all Christians are disciple-makers, how much more should pastors/elders lead the way in doing the same in nurturing disciples toward Christ likeness. This is where the relationship of the pastor to other men is crucial. Pastors are to set the example of what it means to disciple men for spiritual leadership. To borrow John's terminology, "fathers" have the responsibility to disciple "young men," as young men would "little children" (1 John 2:12–14).

Jesus spoke of the "yoke" of his discipleship: "Take my yoke upon you, and learn from Me, for I am gentle and humble in heart; and you shall find rest for your souls. For my yoke is easy, and my load is light" (Matt. 11:29–30, emphasis added). Elsewhere He said, "I gave you an example that you also should do as I did to you" (John 13:15). In exhorting believers in Ephesus to live in righteousness and not as they had lived before, Paul wrote, "You did not learn Christ in this way" (Eph. 4:20, emphasis added). Regarding humility, Paul reminded the Philippians, "Have this attitude in yourselves which was also in Christ Jesus" (Phil. 2:5).

The mandate from John and Peter. Likewise, Peter reminded his readers that they had "been called for this purpose, since Christ also suffered for you, leaving you an example for you to follow in His steps" (1 Pet. 2:21, emphasis added). The apostle John instructed that "the one who says he abides in Him ought himself to walk in the same manner as He walked" (1 John 2:6; cf. 3:24; 4:13–15; 2 John 9; 3 John 11).

PRACTICING

The writer to the Hebrews tells his readers to be "imitators of those who through faith and patience inherit the promises" (Heb. 6:12; cf. 13:7, 9).

The mandate from Paul. Paul also exemplifies the pastor's mandate to disciple-making. He wrote the Corinthians, "I exhort you therefore, be imitators of me" (1 Cor. 4:16). It was not simply Paul they were to imitate, however, because he later wrote, "Be imitators of me, just as I also am of Christ" (1 Cor. 11:1, emphasis added). Further, he exhorted the Ephesians to "be imitators of God, as beloved children" (Eph. 5:1). He encouraged the brethren in Philippi to "join in following my example, and observe those who walk according to the pattern you have in us" (Phil. 3:17). He also told them, "The things you have learned and received and heard and seen in me, practice these things" (Phil. 4:9). That is why the Thessalonians were such an encouragement to Paul: "You also became imitators of us and of the Lord, having received the word in much tribulation with the joy of the Holy Spirit, so that you became an example to all the believers in Macedonia and in Achaia" (1 Thess. 1:6–7; cf. 2:14, 3:7).

Of course, one of the best-known passages conveying the principle of making disciples, especially for pastors, is 2 Tim. 2:2: "And the things which you have heard from me in the presence of many witnesses, these entrust to faithful men, who will be able to teach others also."

Commenting on this verse, Adams has written,
> Men who qualify for the work of ministry are men who can keep the gospel torch burning brightly, so that they are able to pass it on (undimmed) to those who follow.... The people that Paul has in mind are men who "have what it takes" from God to do the work of the ministry. They are men with the gifts who have learned to use them skillfully in the work of shepherding" (Jay Adams, 1975).

147

And they receive much of their skill by being discipled by other godly men. "Paul sees the whole Christian life as a recapitulation of the existence of Jesus and hence as an exercise of what other authors call discipleship." (Wilkins, Following the Master, 306). Discipling as a mandate in the church is nowhere better summed up than in Rev. 14:4, where the 144,000 "follow the Lamb wherever He goes."

The evidence from the Old Testament and the New is clear: All believers, especially pastors/elders and other church leaders, are to make disciples of Jesus Christ. The question is, "What is the best way to implement this mandate?" The answer, of course, is to follow the method employed by Christ Himself!

## Christ's Method for Discipling

The best method for discipling others is that of the Master discipler. Faithful pastors should look to Him to discover a methodology. When they do so, they will discover four key principles followed by Jesus; principles that when applied, will revolutionize their making of disciples. The most succinct expression of those principles is in Mark 3:13–15, "And he went up to the mountain and summoned those whom He Himself wanted, and they came to Him. And He appointed twelve, that they might be with Him, and that He might send them out to preach, and to have authority to cast out the demons."

## Prayerful Meditation

The first principle Jesus used was that of prayerful meditation. Though Mark only says that Jesus "went up to the mountain" (v. 13), Luke 6:12–13 says plainly that "He went off to the mountain to pray, and He spent the whole night in prayer to God. And when day came, He called His disciples to Him." Somewhere on the west side of the Sea of Galilee, Jesus Christ was praying for the Father's guidance in choosing His disciples. This was no insignificant task in the life of our Lord. This decision would affect not only the coming age of the

PRACTICING

church, but also the entire course of history! The suggestion that Jesus—being God in human flesh—did not need to pray (as some have suggested) since He already knew the perfect will of God, questions the very integrity of Jesus Himself. Mark records explicitly that Jesus did pray! He is the God-Man, but He desired to commune with His heavenly Father in order to make a God-honoring choice.

The choice was a monumental commitment, and the Lord faithfully bathed His decision in prayer. In his classic, The Example of Jesus Christ, Stalker has written,

We find Him [Jesus] engaged in special prayer just before taking very important steps in life. One of the most important steps He ever took was the selection from among His disciples of the Twelve who were to be His apostles. It was an act on which the whole future of Christianity depended; and what was He doing before it took place? "It came to pass in those days that He went into a mountain to pray, and continued all night in prayer to God, and, when it was day He called unto Him His disciples, and of them He chose twelve, whom He also named apostles." It was after this night-long vigil, that He proceeded to the choice which was to be so momentous for Him, and for them, and for all the world. There was another day for which, we are told, He made similar preparation. It was that on which He first informed His disciples that He was to suffer and die. Thus it is evident, that, when Jesus had a day of crisis or difficult duty before Him, He gave Himself specially to prayer. Would it not simplify our difficulties if we attacked them in the same way? It would infinitely increase the intellectual insight with which we try to penetrate a problem and the power of the hand we lay upon duty. The wheels of existence would move far more smoothly and our purposes travel more surely to their aims, if every morning we reviewed beforehand the duties of the day with God." (James Stalker, 1980).

The principle of Christ's prayerful meditation for the selection of His disciples is obvious. If a pastor is going to fulfill the

PRACTICING

149

mandate of the Great Commission, he must prayerfully meditate on choosing those whom he would devote his available time to nurture. Whether it is someone whom he personally has led to the Master or a believer who needs further nurturing in the faith, his duty is to pray for them. And if Jesus Christ Himself spent all night in prayer for His disciples, how much more should church leaders? Paul commands us to pray without ceasing (1 Thess. 5: 17), and selecting those for discipleship certainly deserves this unceasing attitude of prayer.

Paul's encouragement to pray about everything (Phil. 4:6) no doubt must include the discipling of others (cf. Eph. 6:18). His prayers for his younger associates are numerous in the Pastoral Epistles (e.g., 1 Tim. 1:2; 2:8; 6:21; 2 Tim. 1:2–3; 4:1, 22; Titus 1:4; 3:15).

When Jesus Christ prayed for His own, He set a tremendous example, especially for pastors. He gave His disciples an example by choosing them prayerfully.

## Careful Selection

The second principle from Jesus' example is careful selection, as Mark 3:13 indicates: "[He] summoned those whom He Himself wanted, and they came to Him."

Historically, Jesus Christ commanded men to follow Him. The pastor committed to discipling others can have three distinct assurances in implementing this process. First, he has the assurance that Christ has commanded those whom He wants for discipleship. In general, Matt. 28:18–20 guarantees the making of disciples, because Christ commanded it, and what He commands, His grace will accomplish. The book of Acts shows clearly that Christ promised the empowering of the Holy Spirit to those who were to make disciples (e.g., Acts 1:8; 4:7–8, 31–33; 6:8). It also shows the result (e.g., Acts 2:41, 47; Acts 6:7; 8:12). This is also a great promise to rest on in the process of making disciples.

PRACTICING

Second, those whom Christ summons will be "those whom He Himself" wants (Mark 3:13). This attests to His real sovereignty in salvation and sanctification. Morgan has rightly observed,

> This word suggests self-determining sovereignty, choice based upon reason within personality.... He was entirely uninfluenced by temporary appeals. No appeal that any man might have made to Him would have influenced Him in the least. No protests of inability that any man might have suggested would have changed His purpose. His choosing was choosing from within, the choosing of His own sovereignty; a choosing therefore in which He assumed all responsibility for what He did. (G. Campbell Morgan, 1927).

It is only by the will of God that anyone becomes a disciple of Christ and that anyone receives discipleship training in Christ (John 1:12–13; 3:6; 6:44, 63, 65, 70; 8:36; 10:3–4, 16; 15:5, 16; 1 John 4: 19). Subject to that same sovereignty, spiritual leaders should carefully select and disciple those to whom God chooses to impart eternal life. Just as the apostles led the congregation in selecting servants in Acts 6:1–6, so leaders today must carefully select others to nurture and teach for service in the body of Christ (Eph. 4:11–16). In addition, as Paul instructed Timothy to entrust spiritual truth to faithful men, church leaders should select such men in whom to reproduce spiritual leadership.

The third assurance a pastor can have in careful selection of prospective disciples is in Mark's phrase, "and they came to Him" (Mark 3:13). This shows that though discipling is a matter of Christ's command and sovereignty, obedience will be the result. Likewise, those who respond in obedience to the gospel summons will obviously be the most likely candidates. These will be willing to take up their cross daily (Luke 9:23)12 and will evidence their readiness for discipleship. However, a word of caution is in order.

PRACTICING

Eims has warned, "Whoever is thinking about or is now involved in a ministry of making disciples ... Should think soberly about this matter of selection. It is much easier to ask a man to come with you than to ask him to leave if you learn, much to your chagrin and sorrow, that you have chosen the wrong man." '(Leroy Eims, 1970).

The chooser must, therefore, be sober and vigilant in his choice. The principle of careful selection was Jesus' method of identifying men to propagate God's kingdom. Church leaders must not forget that men, not programs, are the method of Jesus. Eims has cautioned,

I have watched men catch the vision of reaching the world for Christ. I have caught this vision, and have dedicated my life to this grand and glorious aim. But I have seen some men become so goal-oriented that to achieve their goals they roughly shoulder their way past people who need help and encouragement.

But what is our objective? What are our goals? When we all get to heaven it will all be vividly and pointedly clear. We will find only people in heaven. There will be no committee notes, no scholarly papers on intriguing themes, no lengthy studies, memos, or surveys. People are the raw material of heaven. If we become enamored with projects, goals, and achievements, and never lend a hand to people along the way; and if we say, "Doing this will not help me accomplish my objective," what are we really thinking about? Self! Exactly opposite to the lifestyle of Jesus Christ.

Similarly, Hull says,

Most Christians believe that men are indeed the method of Jesus, but precious few are willing to invest their lives by putting all their eggs in that one basket. Believing this people-oriented philosophy and practicing it are entirely different matters. A large problem in Christendom is that we don't want to take the risk or the time to invest in the lives of people, even though this was a fundamental part of Jesus' ministry. We fear, that the basket is really a trap to ensnare us (Bill Hull , 1984). In his classic work, The Training of The Twelve, Bruce summa-

PRACTICING

rizes this matter of careful selection:

> Why did Jesus choose such men?... If He chose rude, un-
> learned, humble men it was not because He was animat-
> ed by any petty jealousy of knowledge, culture, or good
> birth. If any rabbi, rich man, or ruler had been willing
> to yield himself unreservedly to the service of the king-
> dom, no objection would have been taken to him on ac-
> count of his acquirements, possessions, or titles.... The
> truth is, that Jesus was obliged to be content with fish-
> ermen, and publicans, and quondam zealots, for apos-
> tles. They were the best that could be had. Those who
> deemed themselves better were too proud to become
> disciples, and thereby they excluded themselves from
> what all the world now sees to be the high honor of be-
> ing the chosen princes of the kingdom.... He preferred
> devoted men who had none of these advantages to un-
> devoted men who had them all. And with good reason;
> for it mattered little, except in the eyes of contemporary
> prejudice, what the social position or even the previous
> history of the twelve had been, provided they were spir-
> itually qualified for the work to which they were called.
> What tells ultimately is, not what is without a man, but
> what is within (A. B. Bruce, 1988).

## Purposeful Association

Mark tells of a third crucial principle for disciplers: spending purposeful time with disciples. Mark 3:14 notes that Jesus
"appointed twelve, that they might be with Him." He says very
plainly that Jesus Christ appointed His disciples for the very
purpose of being with Him. The Greek text clause, hina ōsin
meta autou, could mean, "For the purpose" (or "so," or even
"with the result") "that they be with Him." Acts 4:13 later records the fruit of the apostles' time spent with Christ: "As they
[the rulers, elders and scribes] observed the confidence of Peter and John, and understood that they were uneducated and

untrained men, they were marveling, and began to recognize them as having been with Jesus" (emphasis added). The time with Jesus was not only for the purpose of growing and learning under His teaching, but for fellowship and refreshment through His modeling and example. On one occasion, after preaching and teaching, Jesus said, "'Come away by yourselves to a lonely place and rest awhile.' (For there were many people coming and going, and they did not even have time to eat.) And they went away in the boat to a lonely place by themselves" (Mark 6:31–32).

Any effective pastoral ministry will emphasize spending valuable, Christ-honouring time with those who will eventually follow their pastor by entering the ministry. Paul's heart for Timothy was filled with a desire to have fellowship together in the things of the Lord. He said in 1 Tim. 3:14 that he was "hoping to come to [Timothy] before long." Then in 2 Tim. 1:4, he said that he was to see Timothy and "be filled with joy." Paul pleaded with Timothy to "make every effort to come to me soon" (2 Tim. 4:9) and to "make every effort to come before winter" (v. 21). This was not simply a fellowship to meet Paul's needs, but also a time of mutual refreshment and instruction. Paul had such a bond with his disciples! The following describes the occasion after he had discipled the elders of Ephesus for some years and knew they might not see him again: "When he had said these things, he knelt down and prayed with them all. And they began to weep aloud and embraced Paul, and repeatedly kissed him, grieving especially over the word which he had spoken, that they should see his face no more" (Acts 20:36–38). What pathos between Paul and his men!

The structure of such times spent together is flexible, of course, but the point is this: One cannot truly influence those he does not spend time with. If a pastor is going to reproduce himself in the lives of others, it will result from a purposeful association of spiritual fellowship and biblical nurturing. In another context, Whitney writes,

If you suddenly realized you had no more time, would

PRACTICING

you regret how you have spent your time in the past and how you spend it now? The way you have used your time can be a great comfort to you in your last hour. You may not be happy with some of the ways you used your time, but won't you be pleased then for all the times of Spirit-filled living, for all occasions when you have obeyed Christ? Won't you be glad then for those parts of your life that you spent in the Scriptures, prayer, worship, evangelism, serving, fasting, etc., for the purpose of becoming more like the One before whom you are about to stand in judgment (John 5:22–29)

The pastoror leader who is  spending time with Christ will have a profound discipling influence on the ones he/she spends time with. As the leader encourages them to spend time with him in the Word of God, spiritual fruit will abound. This will also result in the accrual of fruit in the people the leader disciples will ultimately influence. It is impossible to overemphasize the principle of purposeful association. To the degree that a leader and his/her prospective disciples spend time together and with Christ, they will reap a plentiful harvest of Christ likeness to the glory of God (cf. Rom. 8:29).

**Powerful Proclamation**

The final aspect in making disciples is powerful proclamation: "And that he might send them out to preach, and to have authority to cast out the demons" (Mark 3:14–15). As Jesus purposed to spend time with His disciples, so He also purposed for them to go out and preach with authority. The Greek construction in verse 14 (the use of a hina purpose clause) is similar to the previous phrase and shows distinctly that Jesus' plan was to disciple these men in order to send them out to preach the gospel with power.

The principle for contemporary application is crucial. Pastors or leader do not simply spend time with others without that association turning outward. This ultimately is the point of discipleship: their disciples make other disciples, and so on.

PRACTICING

Discipleship reaches into the domain of darkness and brings people into the kingdom of light; this is the whole purpose of discipleship. As preachers proclaim the powerful gospel, God makes disciples who will in turn proclaim that same powerful gospel to others. The discipling chain continues unbroken until the day of Jesus Christ.

An implicit principle also emerges from the text. Jesus discipled His men to preach with authority. He purposed to teach them about how to preach (kērussein, to "herald" with a commission to proclaim accurately the prescribed message) and to exercise authority (exousian, "power") in their world. Our calling, too, is to preach and live a righteous life with power in a godless world. Our discipling, then, must include a teaching and an exemplification of how to live the truth in Jesus' name. No other means is available to manifest such a transformed, Christlike life in an un-Christlike culture. The legacy we leave in and through the lives of others we disciple will be powerful and lasting.

## The Disciple-Making Imperative

This chapter has endeavored to show that discipleship and disciple-making are not an option; they are a clear command from Scripture. One summary of the mandate's pervasiveness is: The consensus in the history of the church—ancient and modern—is that the concept of discipleship is apparent everywhere in the New Testament, from Matthew through Revelation.

Our role as pastors (every member is a minister/pastor) also demands that we be disciplers. We cannot be pulpiteers who preach at our people but have no involvement in their lives. The process only begins with the proclamation of Scripture. It finds its real fruition across the entire spectrum of the shepherd's work—feeding, leading, cleaning, bandaging, protecting, nurturing, and every other aspect of a tender shepherd's loving care. This is the process of discipling.

Jesus said that every disciple, when fully trained, will be just like his teacher (Luke 6:40). That places a very heavy weight of responsibility on the discipler to be like his Master, Jesus Christ. We cannot demand that men and women follow us unless, like Paul, we can confidently say that we are imitators of Christ (1 Cor. 11:1). Certainly any man who falters at this point has no business in the pastorate. Moreover, anyone who is not discipling others is abdicating a primary responsibility of his calling. The pastor's calling is to preach, but he cannot be merely an orator—talking at people but never really ministering to them on a personal level. The pastor is called to exhort and instruct, but he cannot be just a professional counselor—dispensing spiritual wisdom from across a desk and apart from holding people accountable. The pastor must lead, but he cannot become a full-time administrator—bogged down with paperwork and business, forgetting that the church is people. For God has not called us to be just a professional pastors; He has called us to be disciple-makers.

PRACTICING

157

# DISCIPLESHIP PROCESS REPORT

Illustration No.8

| 16 | Becomes Christlike | POST-CONVERSION |
|---|---|---|
| 15 | Observes a regular personal devotions and prayer | |
| 14 | Uses his/her spiritual gifts in local church ministry | |
| 13 | Personal finances are based on biblical stewardship | |
| 12 | Accepts and is working toward God's design for the family and home | |
| 11 | Actively shares his/her faith | |
| 10 | Participates in discipleship training | |
| 9 | Faithfully participates in church worship, study groups, or Sabbath School classes | |
| 8 | Publicly acknowledges faith/conversion (in church or among friends) | |
| S | Salvation/conversion experience. Accepts Christ as Saviour | S |
| 7 | Is willing to repent and accept Christ | PRE-CONVER-SION |
| 6 | Realizes sin keeps him/her from salvation | |
| 5 | Recognizes that Christ is the bridge to God and his/her salvation | |
| 4 | Realizes he/she is a sinner | |
| 3 | Believes he/she is responsible to God | |
| 2 | Has faith that there is a Supreme Being | |
| 1 | Has only a superficial awareness of God | |

NAME:_____

ADDRESS: _____

_____

Tel. no: _____ (Mobile) _____

Additional Notes

Taken from Larry Gilbert, Team Evangelism (Lynchburg, Va: Church Growth Institute)

# ORGANIZATIONAL CHARTS FOR RESTRUCTURING OTHER DEPARTMENTS

**Illustration No: 9** *Below: Proposed areas of responsibilities for Outreach coordinator -Reporting to Evangelism coordinator*

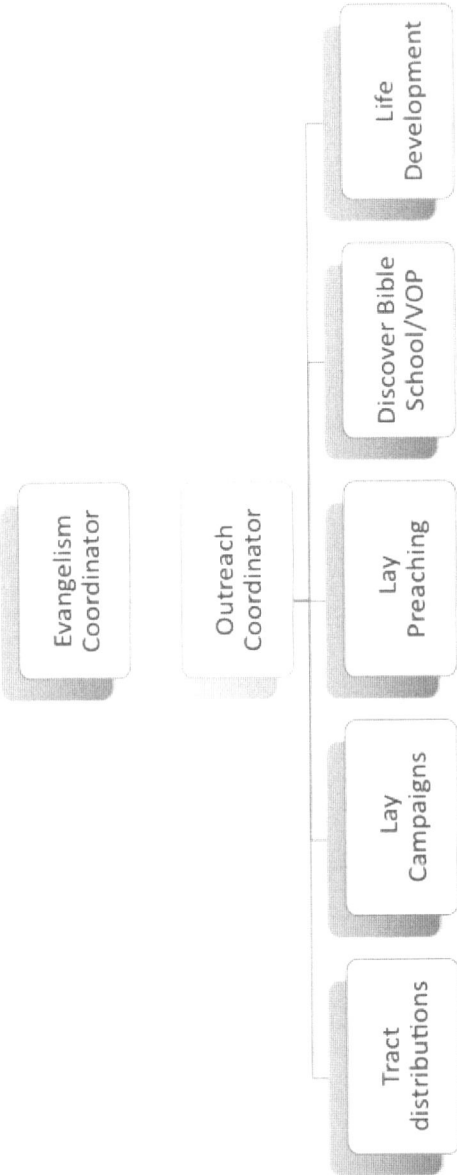

**Illustration No: 10** *Below: Assimilation Process for Visitors- Under the management of Outreach Leadership (Evangelism Department).*

## ASSIMILATION PROCESS – OUTREACH TO VISITORS

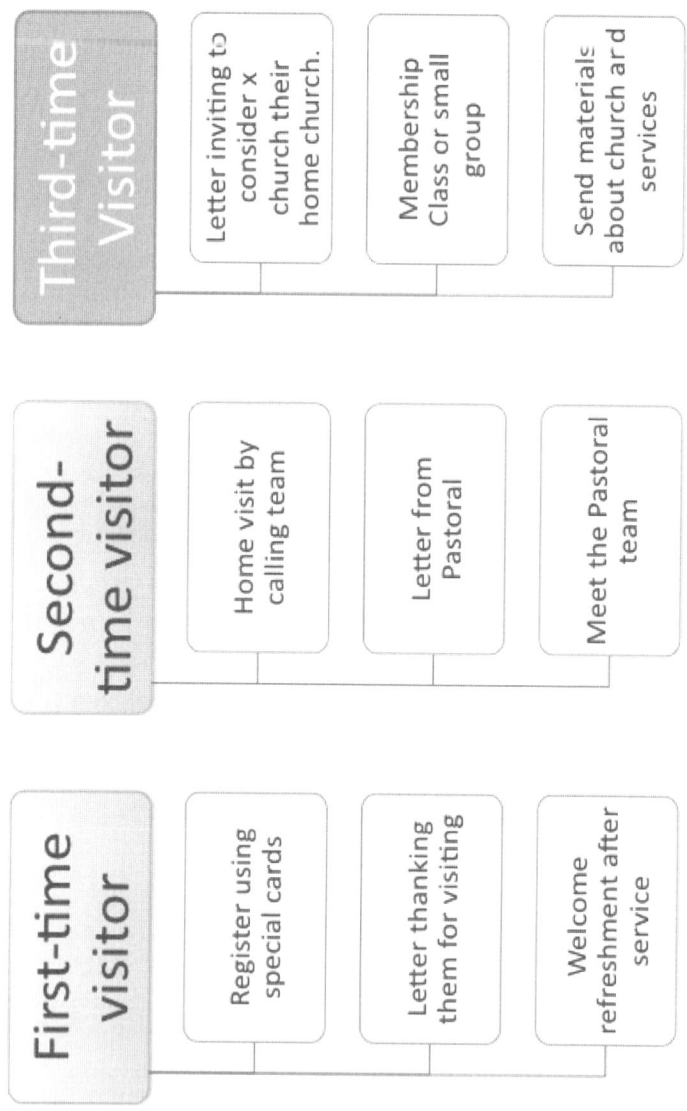

### First-time visitor

- Register using special cards
- Letter thanking them for visiting
- Welcome refreshment after service

### Second-time visitor

- Home visit by calling team
- Letter from Pastoral
- Meet the Pastoral team

### Third-time Visitor

- Letter inviting to consider x church their home church.
- Membership Class or small group
- Send materials about church and services

**Illustration No: 11** *Below: Proposed areas of responsibilities for Inreach coordinator -Reporting to Evangelism coordinator*

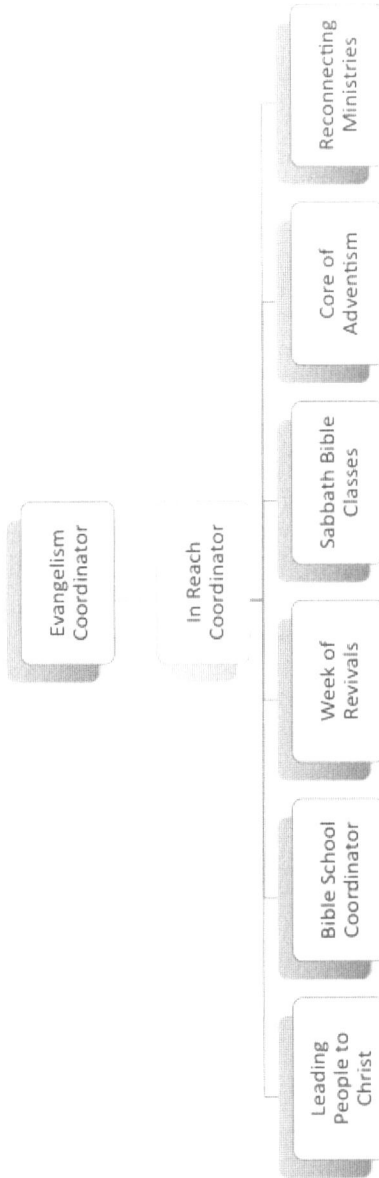

EVANGELISM DEPT AND NEW INREACH COORDINATOR

Evangelism Coordinator

In Reach Coordinator

- Leading People to Christ
- Bible School Coordinator
- Week of Revivals
- Sabbath Bible Classes
- Core of Adventism
- Reconnecting Ministries

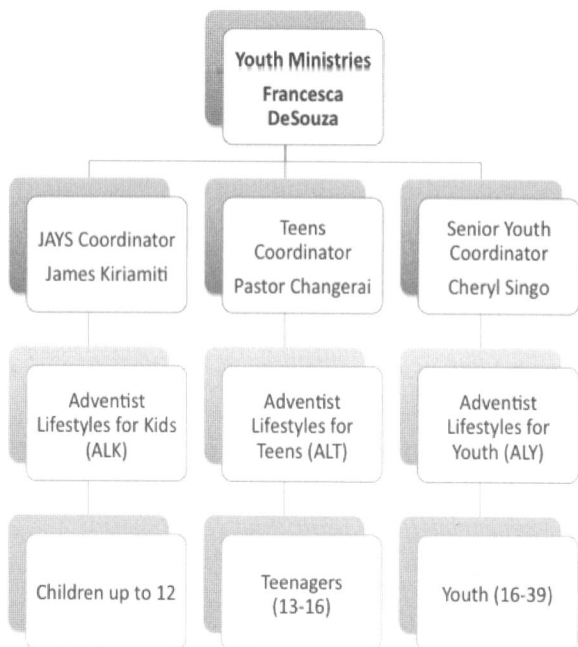

**Illustration No: 12** - *Youth Ministries and Sub-departments for Strategically planning for For growth. JAYS = Junior Adventists Youth Society with the mission of lifestyle development.*

2nd September 2006 - AM

## ROOMS ALLOCATIONS

| Date | Children | Dressing Room | Crew Room | | | Platform Party | Prayer Room | Health Lecture | Stage Manager(s) |
|---|---|---|---|---|---|---|---|---|---|
| 3rd September Morning | Saturday | Committee Room 4 | Committee Room 2 & Changing Rm | | | Courtyard Room & Changing Room | Committee Room 3 & Changing Rm | Bar Area | P. Boldeau, A. Burrell & SAT |

Note 1: Small Hall for Children AND OVERFLOW ROOM.---- PA TECHNICIANS AND VISUAL - Please set up on Friday

| Roll no. | Start | End | Item: Description of Activity | Artist | Type of Activity | Musical Support type | Lighting | Title | On Projection Screen |
|---|---|---|---|---|---|---|---|---|---|
| 001 | 10.00.00 | 10.01.00 | Host Welcome | Susan & Richard | Talk | Musicians | Rostrum | Welcome | Welcome to E T P |
| 002 | 10.01.00 | 10.04.00 | Powering up in Prayer | Ss Nash | Prayer | Background | Rostrum | Prayer | Prayer request announced |
| 002S | 10.04.30 | 10.05.00 | Re-set Stage (platform) | Technicians | None | Background | None | Take off pulpit | Praise n worship ready |
| 003 | 10.05.30 | 10.40.00 | SABBATH SCHOOL | Pastor DeSilva | Talk | Study | Talk | Sabbath School | Bible |
| 003S | 10.41.00 | 10.45.00 | Re-set Stage (platform) | Technicians | None | Background | None | Pulpit on, stands off, tidy up. | Logo |
| 004 | 10.45.30 | 11.20.00 | Praise and Worship including Offerings | Praise Team | Singing | Music | Singers | Pastor N David | Songs |
| 005 | 11.20.00 | 11.22.00 | Hosts intro Pearson & Song - dynamic | Susan & Richard | Talking | Background | Talk | Host | Camera |
| 006 | 11.22.30 | 11.28.30 | Special Music (group) | Kimberley | Singing | Musicians | Singers | Music item 2 | Logo |
| 007 | 11.28.30 | 12.10.00 | Main Presentation Dr W Pearson | Dr Pearson | Preaching | | Rostrum | "Jesus is knocking at your door" | Camera |
| 008 | 12.10.05 | 12.15.30 | Special Music (appeal song) | Denice Wint | Singing (Soloist) | Musicians | Singers | | Logo |
| 009 | 12.16.00 | 12.28.00 | Praise & Worship | Praise Team | Singing | Musicians | Singers | "Jesus, Jesus" | Theme Song |
| 010 | 12.28.30 | 12.40.50 | Intro to Baptism Candidates | Dr S Thomas | Talk | Musicians | Praise Team Kim | Support | Songs |
| 011 | 12.41.00 | 12.47.00 | Commitment to Serve in vows | Pastor S McKenzie | Talk | Musicians | Praise Team Kim | Support | Vows |
| 012 | 12.47.00 | 13.30.00 | BAPTISM | Pastors | Baptism | Praise Team | Pool | Baptism | |
| 013 | 13.31.00 | 13.45.00 | Praise Team/Pearson | Praise Team | Singing | Musicians | Singers | "Jesus, Jesus" | Theme Song |

**Illustration 14:** Above: An example of an Evangelistic Running Order (used for Experienced the Power with Walter Pearson in 2005). The schedule provide detailed information in order to have an effective service.

# Job Descriptions for Evangelistic Meetings

# JOB DESCRIPTIONS
# FOR EVANGELISTIC MEETINGS

### Understanding the Purpose of Campaigns
### Job Descriptions

Like every workplace, a campaign has a number of jobs to be done. It is always better to develop position descriptions so that the leaders can:

1.  Clarify expectations. A well-defined position can communicate what is needed in any job, how a person in ministry will be evaluated (whether formally or informally), and how leaders will know the work is getting done.
2.  Set boundaries. There's a difference between expecting a person to do a few things well (very efficient) and doing a little of everything (very inefficient).

Job descriptions can set important boundaries between workers so that they are not taking over other people's work—or not giving the best effort to their own work.

3.  Define lines of authority. People want to know to whom they are accountable, and why. Workers also will be less likely to send mixed signals about whose direction to follow, and at what point the supervisor takes charge.
4.  Eliminate work and ministry conflicts. With clearer boundaries and lines of authority, the likelihood that people will move into conflict is greatly reduced.

Workers will respect and honour their co-workers and understand how each of them must be part of a team to advance the Lord's work.

**PEOPLE**

## Campaign Coordinator

1. Oversees all committees.
2. Ensures that all tasks are completed on time.
3. Ensures that staffing schedules are completed.
4. Should be a pastor or someone appointed by the pastor and can work closely with the pastor.

## Venue Coordinator

1. Responsible for the meeting hall or church
2. Ensures that hall or church is clean, attractive, and inviting.
3. Oversees such things as lighting, signage, temperature regulation, emergency procedures, etc.
4. Checks rest rooms, foyer, and seating areas for attractiveness and cleanliness
5. May have a committee of several people to assist in the details of this important responsibility

## Treasurer

1. Keeps track of expenses and income for the campaign
2. Oversees security of funds and accountability for those who collect and count offerings
3. Pay invoices in a timely manner
4. Ensures that all invoices paid are legitimate and in accordance with contracts
5. Requires and keeps receipts for all expenditures
6. Follows approved procedures for handling money as established by conference audit policy
7. Never fewer than two people counting money
8. Counting of money to take place in a secure location, away from prying eyes
9. Banking conducted in a timely manner
10. Expenses carefully tracked against campaign budget
11. Receipts and reports provided to the campaign committee

## Advertising and Communication Coordinator

1. Responsible for ordering an advertising package
2. Ensures that advertising goes out in a timely manner
3. Includes such things as handbills, door hangers, newspaper ads, radio/TV ads, personal invitations, and the flow of information to those in attendance in order to update them on upcoming topics

## Registration Coordinator

1. Staffs and schedules registration table
2. Orders registration materials
3. Sets up registration area
4. Delivers nightly registration information to the Interest Coordinator
5. Responsible for sermon outlines, attendance rewards, and other materials your church wishes to provide to attendees
6. Coordinates with and shares information with Interest File Coordinator and Visitation Coordinator. If someone is hesitant to register, share these reasons for registering:
7. We are providing free study materials to those who register
8. We are offering books to those who attend a certain number of nights
9. During the course of the seminar, we will be providing free update materials to those who are registered.

## Interest/Prospect File Coordinator

1. This is a crucial position for the success of the campaign. This position can ensure that no attendee falls through the cracks and that every interest if properly followed up.

PEOPLE

169

2. Keeps list of interests
3. Tracks names and oversees follow up
4. Coordinates with pastor to rate level of interests
5. Keeps attendance records
6. Works closely with Registration coordinator in ensure that all guests are registered
7. Recruits data-entry volunteers to help enter names into a database
8. Establishes a private data-entry location at the hall or church
9. Prints nightly attendance reports and provides them to the visitation committee
10. Equips registration tables

### Head Greeter

1. Reports to Hospitality Coordinator
2. Schedules greeters well in advance and confirm those on duty each night
3. Presents a greeter schedule to the Hospitality coordinator
4. Sends written notice to each greeter of their schedule

### Greeters

1. Visitors receive their first impression of your church from the greeters. Greeters set the stage for everything that happens. A good greeter is invaluable for any church or evangelistic meeting since most people decide whether or not they will return during the first 15 minutes of their visit.
2. Two greeters are to be stationed at each entrance to the church
3. Greeters should attempt to attend every night of the meetings in order to be able to recognise the guests and call them by name.
4. Greeters should be well dressed and always wear a

PEOPLE

smile. They will greet each guest warmly and have no fear of speaking to strangers.

5. Smile, shake hands, and speak in a friendly manner to visitors while attempting to learn their name.
6. Direct everyone to the registration table, including church members. Explain that they will receive a free Bible and seminar materials if they register.
7. Be willing to answer questions but do not engage in doctrinal discussions with the guests. Let them know that this subject will be addressed during the course of the seminar, or direct them to the pastor.
8. Refrain from doctrinal language. Do not greet people with "Happy Sabbath" on Friday or Saturday night, even after the subject has been presented. Simply befriend the guests and let the Holy Spirit work on their hearts.
9. Don't huddle with other evangelistic personnel or church members for a visit. Greet church members as warmly as you greet guests, and urge them to go inside and take a seat so that the lobby is not congested.
10. Be willing to help at the registration desk and hand out materials. You may also be asked to collect Bibles at the end of the meeting.
11. Become well acquainted with the hall or church in order to direct people to washrooms, children's ministries series, etc.

### Head Usher

1. Recruits and schedules ushers each evening
2. Ensures that an adequate number of ushers are in place to meet the needs of the meeting each evening. The master schedule should include phone numbers for each usher.
3. Makes a master copy of the schedule for ushers and makes it available to the Campaign Coordinator

PEOPLE

**Ushers**

1. Should be dressed in a manner that makes a good impression on guests. While a jacket and tie are suggested, final decisions on dress code should be made by each church as is appropriate for local customs. Ladies who serve as ushers should also remember to dress professionally and modestly.
2. Ushers should be prepared to deal with guests in a friendly, polite manner, remembering that they are our guests.
3. Honour those who have reserved-seating tickets by showing them to the reserved seat section. Seats should be held until 10 minutes prior to the beginning of the programme.
4. Assist guest in finding a seat when the hall or church becomes crowded.
5. Assists late arriving guests in finding a seat.
6. Know the location of rest rooms, registration desks, and children ministries programme facilities and be prepared to direct guests.
7. At the direction of the Venue Coordinator, ushers will set up the hall prior to the meetings as well as tidying up after each meeting.
8. Take up the offering when it is called for. When the offering appeal is made, ushers should immediately walk to their assigned section with offering buckets or offering plates. Collecting the offering should not take more than one or two minutes.
9. During the presentation/sermon, two ushers should quietly take count of the audience. Count should include everyone in the audience as well as staff. A separate count should be taken of the children in the children's ministries programme rooms. The number in attendance is to be given to the Campaign Coordinator each night.
10. Be prepared to dispense and collect decision cards.

PEOPLE

## Usher/Greeters Coordinator

**The usher/greeter coordinator is responsible to:**
1. Arrange for the correct number of ushers and greeters.
2. Prepare a seating chart of the venue, and assign ushers based on one per four or five rows of attendees.
3. Provide offering containers (one per row); quiz envelopes, pens/pencils, decision cards, etc. for ushers.

**Train ushers to:**
1. Help people find seats.
2. Make friends and give a good first impression.
3. Distribute and collect quiz envelopes, decision cards and pens/pencils.
4. Handle possible disturbances.
5. Take up offerings (one bucket per row, so that it will be quick).
6. Bring in extra chairs if necessary.
7. Watch for need of climate control (people putting on sweaters or fanning themselves.)

**Instruct greeters about:**
- Registration process.
- Making a good first impression.

8. Arrange for someone to be at the venue each evening before the meeting in time to get temperature controls adjusted and have things unlocked (at least an hour before the meeting).
9. Arrange for decision cards to be provided for ushers on evenings that Pastor X calls for decision cards.
10. Make sure that the appropriate people are ready in the front if a call is made for people to come forward. They will need to greet them, pray for them and get their names.
11. A decision must be made as to whether a nursery will be provided, or whether a program will be offered to

PEOPLE

children. Some may choose to offer both. Whatever decision is made, all areas of children's ministries must be adequately staffed and thoroughly planned. This area is one of the most important areas for the meetings. If this is done well, the meetings will benefit greatly. If done poorly, the meetings will suffer and children will be the real losers.

12. Research indicates that the most effective area of evangelism today is with children ages five through 12. It is during these years that a lasting decision for Christ is most likely to be made. Do not view children's ministries as merely baby-sitting. This is prime-time evangelism! Use this as an opportunity to introduce children to Jesus.

**Children's Ministries Committee Coordinator**

1. Assists the Pastor and Campaign Coordinator in recruiting and screening Children's Ministries volunteers. It is essential that only those who can be demonstrated to be "safe" to work with children be used in this area.
2. Organise volunteers into teams that will serve on a rotating basis.
3. Organise and circulates a nightly schedule for children's ministries workers or teams.
4. Appoints a leader for each team who will be responsible for the programme on the night scheduled.
5. Holds an organisational meeting in order to plan each night of the programme in advance.
6. Inventories materials that will be needed and provides adequate supplies.
7. Ensure that adequate staff are present each night of the meetings. This includes teachers, leaders, musicians, as well as those who can accompany a child to the rest room as well as someone who can locate a parent in the meeting in the case of an emergency. Children should not be taken into the meeting. Parents are to be located

in the meeting and brought to their children. This will
be less disruptive of the meetings.

8. Provide a method of security, tagging each child with
first and last name, and a number. A tag with a corresponding number is given to the parent or guardian.
Children may only be released to someone who has the
correct number.

9. Prepare a handout for parents to explain your system
of security and reassures parents that their children
will be well cared for.

10. Make every attempt to keep children as happy as possible.

## Children Ministries Workers

1. Have at least one adult for every seven children at the
event.

2. Members will oversee activities for each evening of the
meeting, and will contact the committee head should a
problem be encountered.

3. Team members will prepare a schedule for each nights
programme and work together to ensure that everything goes well.

4. Will assist in tagging children with first and last names,
as well as a number. A corresponding number should
be given to each parent.

5. Ensures that no child is released to anyone who does
not possess the correct number.

6. Makes certain that no children's ministries worker is
ever alone with a child.

7. Ensures the safety of each child.

8. Does everything possible to make certain that each
child is happy and enjoys the evening.

PEOPLE

## Music Coordinator

1. Direct the planning and conducting of music within the campaign, especially those portions of the worship services that pertain to music.
2. Coordinate the music programmes with the campaign calendar and emphases of the campaign.
3. Work with the Campaign Coordinators in determining the goals of the campaign overall music programme.
4. Assist the Pastor and the rest of the campaign team in planning the services of the campaign.
5. Be responsible for the selection of music, particularly hymns and solos.
6. Coordinate the performance schedules of music groups and individuals within the campaign.
7. Supervise maintenance of and additions to musicians, singers, and equipment necessary for the campaign.
8. Keep informed on current music methods, materials, utilizing them where appropriate.
9. Prepare the music budget for the campaign
10. Music Department to be recommended to the campaign finance committee.
11. Expand and enhance the breadth and depth of the choir's range of music, using an ever-increasing number of genres of music employed for the services.
12. Seek to involve choir members in the life and witness of the campaign beyond the activities of the choir.

## Audiovisual

1. Reports to Platform coordinator
2. Provides sufficient microphones
3. Ensures that a supply of batteries is kept on hand
4. Runs the equipment (test them), video projectors, or other equipment.
5. Ensures that DVD or videotaped copies of sermons are used as loans for those who miss meetings.

**PEOPLE**

6. Plays suitable, soft music if asked to by the Music Coordinator
7. Controls auditorium lighting, stage lights, etc.
8. Arrives at the meeting 30 to 45 minutes prior to the start of the meeting to ensure that equipment is turned on and in working order
9. Meets with the Platform coordinator each night to be familiarized with the evening's programme

## Prayer Coordinator

The prayer coordinator is responsible to:
1. Organise one or more prayer bands. Each prayer band should meet regularly to pray for the upcoming meetings, for members' contacts, and for the church's spiritual readiness.
2. Give at least one short presentation on the power and necessity of prayer before the sermon begins. A bulletin insert or other presentation may be appropriate.
3. Have a special prayer session before the meetings begin.
4. Set up a prayer request box or other system for getting prayer requests from Sermon attendees.
5. During the series, set aside a private room and gather a group each night to pray during the meeting. (A sign-up sheet at church will probably be the easiest way to facilitate this.) Prayer requests can include the speaker, the presence and action of the Holy Spirit, the spiritual welfare of guests (including those who have attended previously), any recognized problems or blessings, and requests that have been turned in.

PEOPLE

# How to Help
# People Make
# Positive Decisions

# 12

# HOW TO HELP PEOPLE
# MAKE POSITIVE DECISIONS [1]

## I. Expect Decisions!

1. Helping people decide to do something about the truths they have been studying and accepting is often the most difficult part of soul- winning. Many individuals are led to study God's Word and believe the truths that are presented, but never take any action to bring their lives into conformity to these teachings.

2. Leading people to decide for something that is often unpopular, out of step with society, and threatening to their financial well-being is not an easy task. It is, indeed, a science and a most vital part of soul winning. The principles and techniques of this science are discussed in this section.

3. Here is our Lord's promise: "When we give ourselves wholly to God, and in our work follow His directions, He makes Himself responsible for its accomplishment." (White, Christ's Object Lessons, 363.)

## II. Practical Principles

### A. Inspired secrets to success

"There is need of coming close to the people by personal effort. If less time were given to sermonizing and more time were

---

[1] *Excerpts from Mark Finley, How To Help People Make Positive Decisions, Hart Research Center, 52.*

spent in personal ministry, greater results would be seen. Accompanied by the:
1. Power of persuasion
2. Power of prayer

Power and love of God ... This work will not, cannot, be without fruit." (White, The Ministry of Healing, 143, 144.) "There are great laws that govern the world of nature, and spiritual things are controlled by principles equally certain. The means for an end must be employed if the desire results are to be attained."

### III. Techniques and Approaches for Leading People to a Decision

### A. Principles for Gaining Decisions

**Be agreeable.** Discuss those features of truth on which you can agree.

"If the worker keeps his heart uplifted in prayer, God will help him to speak the right word at the right time" (White, Gospel Workers, 120.)

"Agree with the people on every point where you can consistently do so" (White, Evangelism, 141.)

**Be alert.** Watch for indications that reveal the trend of the thoughts. Help the individual to develop his own conclusions. Remember—you are building a bridge, so drive down one pile at a time.

"The sacred responsibility rests upon the minister to watch for souls as one that must give an account. He must interest himself in the souls for whom he labours, finding out all that perplexes and troubles them and hin-

**PERSUASION**

181

ders them from walking in the light of the truth." (White, Gospel Workers, 190, 191.)

**Be direct.** Move straight on to your objective. Avoid being sidetracked. Keep the person's thought progression toward the goal, but do not go too fast.

> "The secret of our success and power as a people advocating advanced truth will be found in the making of direct, personal appeals to those who are interested." (White., Advent Review & Sabbath Herald, August 30, 1892.)

> "Many times minds are impressed with tenfold more force by personal appeals than by any other kind of labour" (White, Letter 95, 1896.)

**Be kind and courteous**. Remember that Jesus was always courteous. He never spoke an unkind word. Every morning He was given the tongue of the learned (Isaiah 50:4).
> "He knew 'how to speak a word in season to him that is weary'; for grace was poured upon His lips, that He might convey to men in the most attractive way the treasures of truth" (White, The Desire of Ages, 254.)

> "Into what you say put the spirit and life of Christ" (White, Evangelism, 175.)
> "Put all the Christ-like tenderness and love possible into the voice" (White, Evangelism, 174.)

**Never argue.** It is possible to win the argument and lose the man. A good soul-winner never argues.

> "Satan is constantly seeking to produce effects by rude and violent thrusts; but Jesus found access to minds by the pathway of their most familiar associations. He dis-

turbed as little as possible their accustomed train of thought." (White, Evangelism, 140.)

**Meet objections with Scriptures**. Jesus met arguments of the Pharisees and the temptations of the devil by quoting from the Word of God. To every fresh challenge He could reply, "It is written." In addition, we will find our strength where the Saviour found His.

> "Objections can each be met with a 'Thus saith the Lord'" (White, Letter 95, 1896.)

**The Time for Decision is Now!**

> "Bring them to the point to decide. Show them the importance of the truth; it is life or death. With becoming zeal pull souls out of the fire" (White, Testimonies for the Church, Vol. 1, 152.)

> "Many are convicted of sin, and feel their need of a sin-pardoning Saviour if words are not spoken at the right moment, calling for decision from the weight of evidence already presented, the convicted ones pass on without identifying themselves with Christ, the golden opportunity passes, and they have not  yielded, and they go farther and farther away from the truth" (White, Evangelism, 283.)

**Salvation is in the Present Tense.**

1. "Today if ye will hear His voice harden not your hearts." Hebrews 3:15.
2. "Behold, now is the accepted time; behold, now is the day of salvation." 2 Corinthians 6:2.
3. "Many will be lost while hoping and desiring to be Christians. They do not come to the point of yielding the will to God. They do not now choose to be Christians" (White, Steps to Christ, 48.)

PERSUASION

## Recognize the time factor involved in
## Calling for a decision

1. Decisions must be called for when conviction comes.
2. "When persons who are under conviction are not brought to make a decision at the earliest period possible, there is danger that the conviction will gradually wear away" (White, Evangelism, 298.)
3. Not everyone comes under conviction at the same point. Present Jesus as the One who is calling for their decision.
4. "Talk to souls in peril and get them to behold Jesus upon the cross dying to make it possible for Him to pardon us" (White, Testimonies for the Church, Vol. 6, 67.)

## Acceptance of Christ is essential to all
## Other major decisions

Avoid presenting the church or yourself as calling for decision.

**Employ Scripture as a basis for all appeals.**

1. "Be very careful how you handle the Word, because that Word is to make the decisions with the people. Let the Word cut and not your words" (White, Evangelism, 300.)
2. Clear Scripture appeals carry tremendous force.
3. Employ prayer as a means of calling for decision.
4. Pray for the person to have courage to make a decision.
5. "Pray with these souls, by faith bringing them to the foot of the cross. Carry their minds with your mind and fix the eye of faith where you look upon Jesus, the sin bearer.
6. Get them to look from their poor sinful selves to the Saviour and the victory is won" (White, Testimonies for the Church, Vol. 6.)
7. Ask them to pray, if appropriate.

PERSUASION

### Never close the door on a soul's salvation

The Holy Spirit may wait to bring conviction under circumstances that are more favourable. The individual may not understand the point at issue. Make friends for God, not enemies.

## IV. The Science of Securing Decisions

### A. A Study of How the Mind Works

1. Every gospel worker needs to understand clearly how the human mind works in making a favorable decision.
2. This is basic in securing decisions. This has been pointed out in the instruction from the Spirit of Prophecy.
3. In order to win souls to Jesus there must be "a study of the human mind" (White, Testimonies for the Church, Vol. 4, 67.)

> "There are great laws that govern the world of nature, and spiritual things are controlled by principles equally certain. The means for an end must be employed, if the desired results are to be attained" (White, Testimonies for the Church, Vol. 9, 221.)

### B. Knowledge, Conviction, and Desire Lead to Decisions

1. Decisions stem out of the interplay of knowledge, conviction, and desire in a person's mind. This is true according to Scripture and science. When a person's knowledge, conviction, and desire in reference to a given subject reach certain intensity, the mind moves into decision and action in regard to it.

2. Since knowledge, conviction, and desire lead to decision, the sermons, the Bible studies, and the personal talks should be an artful interweaving of the factors of desire and conviction in respect to the given subject. This is

PERSUASION

needed for bringing about the requisite interplay of knowledge, conviction, and desire that will result in acceptance, decision, and action.

3.  As we analyze certain Bible texts, we discover that some are especially designed to bring knowledge, others to bring conviction, and still others to bring desire. In addition, the same text has in it the elements of all three. We need to focus on the texts that will implant conviction and at the same time arouse desire for accepting and following God's great principles as we present them in our Bible studies to the student.

### C. The Direct Personal Appeal in Conjunction with Knowledge, Conviction, and Desire

Effective personal work is based on an adherence to a cluster of God-ordained principles, or spiritual laws. One of the most important is the use of the direct, personal appeal. It is the secret of success in dealing with interested people.

"The secret of our success and power as a people advocating advanced truth will be found in making direct, personal appeals to those who are interested, having unwavering reliance upon the Most High" (Advent Review & Sabbath Herald, August 30, 1892.)

**Paul Used the Direct Personal Appeal.** One of the best illustrations of the principles involved in this direct, personal appeal is Paul's appeal to Agrippa, as recorded in Acts 26:22-28.

**Use of the Knowledge of the Word**. Paul prepared the way for making the personal appeal by an effective use of the Word. His appeal was based on the teachings of the Scriptures (Acts 26:22, 23.)

## Personal Experience Creating Desire

1. The appeal should be connected with, or grow out of, the person's own experience and knowledge. Paul used his own testimony as to how he found Christ and what He was to him. What was the reaction to Paul's testimony?
   "The whole company had listened spellbound to Paul's account of his wonderful experiences. The apostle was dwelling upon his favourite theme. None who heard him could doubt his sincerity" (White, Acts of the Apostles, 437.)

**Appeal Directed to Agrippa's Convictions.** Paul directed his appeal to Agrippa's convictions, taking the form of a question. He designed to bring home to Agrippa a realization of his personal responsibility (Acts 26:27, first part). Paul's appeal is concluded by expecting that Agrippa will respond (Acts 26:27, last part). It was an appeal at an opportune moment. Was Agrippa moved? "Deeply affected, Agrippa for the moment lost sight of his surroundings and the dignity of his position. Conscious only of the truths which he had heard, seeing only the humble prisoner standing before him as God's ambassador, he answered involuntarily, 'Almost thou persuaded me to be a Christian'" (White, Acts of the Apostles, 438.)

### VISITATION AND BIBLE STUDY GUIDE

## Difficult Visits

At times an interest will become argumentative. Remember, no one will ever win an argument. Do not allow yourself to be caught up in an argument. Never insult the intelligence of an interest, but instead, try to find areas of agreement and areas where you can affirm his intelligence. Then calmly, present your case for truth.

PERSUASION

Make your answers brief, simple, and calm. Never argue. Never debate. If your interest is hostile, change the subject and come back to it some other time. If you don't have an answer, don't be afraid to admit it. Trying to make up an answer will destroy your credibility. Simply say, "I really don't have an answer to that question.

Give me some time to think about it and I'll see if there is a good answer." Then go find the answer. Remember that you cannot press a person too hard if you have not built a friendship with that person. Relationship is the key. When a friendship is established, it is easier to speak to a person about matters of the soul. If the discussion becomes heated, break off the discussion in order to retain the friendship. The relationship is the key.

Don't spend a great deal of time on any objection. Make your answer brief and simple. Then go on to another subject.

Remember that the first objection is rarely the real issue. Listen more than you talk. Listen to more than the words. Listen to the emotion behind the words. The Holy Spirit will reveal to you the real issue. Then you can proceed.

Truth is logical and makes great sense. When plainly presented in a calm, non-argumentative fashion, it will usually win the day. But even when it does not win, find a place of agreement to end the conversation. Hold on to the relationship. Ultimately, the relationship will be the tool the Holy Spirit uses to bring the interest to Christ. Make certain to speak about the difference Jesus has made in your life. There is no answer for an honest, personal testimony.

PERSUASION

## Major Teachings

All major teachings should be discussed with each interest. However, they need not be discussed all at once.. It is better to allow interests to make a lot of smaller decisions which can help lead to the bigger decision of following Jesus completely. Making smaller decisions along the way will cause them to feel that the main decision of following Jesus is a very natural decision and therefore much easier than it would have been otherwise.

Try not to run ahead of the subjects in the meeting. Trying to run too fast can actually frighten an interest away.

Major decisions that need to be clear in your interest's mind before baptism are:

1. Plan of Salvation
2. Daily Growth in Christ
3. Authority of Scripture
4. Baptism by Immersion
5. Second Coming
6. Sabbath
7. Moral Law
8. State of the Dead
9. Hell
10. Healthful Living
11. Gift of Prophecy

While the church has many more teachings than those included in this list, these are necessary before one joins the church.

PERSUASION

## Baptism

This is where the hard work of building quality relationships pays off. Your interest has now become your brother or sister. You are joint heirs of the Kingdom of God.

There is no sweeter work than that of bringing someone to the decision of baptism. The joy that is experienced in heaven spills over into your heart as you recognize that God has used you as His agent in this beautiful process. **Do not wait until an interest is perfect before baptizing them.** Do not even wait until all of the teachings of the Seventh-day Adventist Church have been accepted. Once the teachings previously listed have been accepted, an individual is ready for baptism. Do not hinder anyone from being baptized once these sacred truths have been accepted.

You may wish to form a baptismal class even before the series starts and certainly during, as well as after it has ended. Certainly by the final evening of the meetings you should be ready to announce that further studies are available for those who wish to follow Christ all the way.

You will conduct these studies using the appropriate baptismal study guides. Include in the campaign meetings, not only those who have already committed for baptism, but also those who are just interested. Keep the door open to as many interests as possible.

Make it clear that your church members are not to attend these classes unless they are helping to organise the classes or unless they bring someone to the classes. Not all of your members will be wise enough not to interfere with what the Holy Spirit wants to accomplish in these studies.

You will want to plan for several meetings to cover the remaining doctrines, since the campaign/outreach tends to be

PERSUASION

short series. We will not have covered all the necessary doctrines. This means that you will need to hold more baptismal meetings.

Have your visitation teams continue to make visits to interest during this time. Again, let the focus be on building relationships and meeting needs. This is also a great opportunity for visitors to share a testimony about what relationship with Christ has meant in their life. If a candidate misses a baptismal class, have the visitors carry the study guide to the candidate at home. They can even offer to go over the guide with the candidate if time permits. If not, offer to drop back by to answer any questions they may have about the topic covered in the guide once they have had a chance to complete the lesson on their own.

Once the classes are complete and all of the teachings have been covered, make sure there are no moral issues, which would prevent a candidate from partaking of baptism, and then schedule a date for the baptism.

You might say something like:

> "Jane, it appears that we have gone over all the essential beliefs and it sounds like you and I pretty much believe the same things. We have a baptism planned for _____, and I can't think of a reason why you shouldn't be a part of it, can you?"

Wait for a response as you continue to smile. Don't speak again until the interest speaks, no matter how long it takes. Allow the Holy Spirit to do His work just now. If an objection is raised, clear it up quickly with your Bible and ask the question again.

If the candidate expresses more reservations or just doesn't want to make a decision right now, don't push too hard. Plead gently, but leave room for a return visit and a maintained friendship.

**PERSUASION**

191

# Sample Evangelistic Materials

# FAMILY FOR LIFE, HEALTH FOR ETERNITY SERIES

## Remedy for Stress

❑ I desire to obey Jesus fully.

❑ I accept the Bible Sabbath as the true Lord's day.

❑ I love Jesus and desire to keep the seventh-day Sabbath holy.

❑ I desire more reading material on the Bible Sabbath.

Name: _____

Address: _____

City: _____

State: _____

Zip/Postcode: _____

Phone: _____

E-mail &iChat _____

Above: Sample Decision (response) card used in the Reading District Evangelistic series.

# FAMILY FOR LIFE,
## HEALTH FOR ETERNITY

## Registration Card

Name: _____

Address: _____

City/Town: _____

County(UK only): _____

Postcode: _____

Email: _____

Phone: _____

☐ 1  ☐ 2  ☐ 3  ☐ 4  ☐ 5  ☐ 6  ☐ 7  ☐ 8  ☐ 9  ☐ 10  ☐ 11  ☐ 12  ☐ 13

☐ 14  ☐ 15  ☐ 16  ☐ 17  ☐ 18  ☐ 19  ☐ 20  ☐ 21  ☐ 22  ☐ 23  ☐ 24  ☐ 25

Sample Registration card used in previous evangelistic series.

# JESUS IS THE LIGHT OF THE WORLD
## Evangelistic Planning Checklist

| Item | Checking Questions | Answer (yes/no) | Remarks |
|------|-------------------|-----------------|---------|
| 001 | What is the purpose of the upcoming ministry event? (Ephesians 4:11-16) | | |
| 002 | Will the evangelist fit the purposes of this campaign? | | |
| 003 | Is the evangelist known as a solid Bible preacher? (Ephesians 4:12-13) | | |
| 005 | Does the evangelist conduct himself or herself as a Christian ambassador for the Lord? (Luke 10:1) | | |
| 006 | Is the evangelist accountable to fellow ministers? (Acts 8:14-24) | | |
| 007 | Does the evangelist refrain from engaging in sensationalism to attract crowds? (Acts 8:9-12) | | |
| 008 | Is the evangelist willing to go to a church when the timing is best for the local congregation? | | |
| 009 | Is the evangelist ethical in all areas of ministry? | | |
| 010 | Does the evangelist do the full "work of the evangelist"? (2 Timothy 4:5) | | |
| 011 | Does the evangelist focus on exalting the name of Jesus Christ? (Acts 8:12) | | |
| 012 | Is the evangelist a personal soul-winner? (Acts 8:25-40) | | |
| 013 | What is the minimum experience level needed for this event? | | |

**Illustration No15** *Above: Checklist for Evangelistic Campaigns. For copies, please e-mail: me at pastorthomas@mac.com*

# JESUS IS THE LIGHT OF THE WORLD
## Evangelistic Planning Checklist

| Item | Checking Questions | Answer (yes/no) | Remarks |
|------|-------------------|-----------------|---------|
| | SELECTING THE SPEAKERS FOR CHURCH EVENTS | | |
| 014 | Years in ministry or church work? | | |
| 015 | The proposed speaker's ability and expertise in the particular event being planned? | | |
| 016 | Knowledge, ability to cope with the particular event, and maturity? | | |
| 017 | 1. The type of event being organized<br>a. Revival?<br>b. Daniel or Revelation Series?<br>c. Family Emphasis Series<br>d. Health Evangelism?<br>e. Lay campaign?<br>f. Church or District Campaign | | |

# JESUS IS THE LIGHT OF THE WORLD
## Evangelistic Planning Checklist

### Preparation Checklist

| Item | Checking Questions | Answer (yes/no) | Remarks |
|---|---|---|---|
| A | **VENUE** | | |
| 004 | Finance set aside for venue? | | |
| 005 | Invoice Received? | | |
| 006 | Invoice Paid? | | |
| 007 | Planning team affirmed decision? | | |
| 008 | Planning in progress for venue layout? | | |
| B | **CAMPAIGN (EVANGELISTIC) SPEAKER** | | |
| 009 | Evangelists Selection Process commenced? | | |
| 010 | Evangelists Selection Process completed? | | |
| 011 | Evangelists Selected? | | |
| 012 | Evangelists confirmed with dates? | | |
| 013 | Evangelists reconfirmed dates)? | | |
| 014 | Evangelists Service Request submitted to Conference/Union etc? | | |
| 015 | Evangelists Service Requested approved? | | |

# JESUS IS THE LIGHT OF THE WORLD
## Evangelistic Planning Checklist

Preparation Checklist

| Item | Checking Questions | Answer (yes/no) | Remarks |
|---|---|---|---|
| **B** | **CAMPAIGN (EVANGELISTIC) SPEAKERS continue** | | |
| 016 | Evangelists terms and conditions agreed? | | |
| 017 | Evangelists flight booked? | | |
| 018 | Evangelists Accommodation booked? | | |
| 019 | Evangelists Dietary requirements confirmed and meal-plan confirmed? | | |
| 020 | Evangelists transportation during meetings confirmed? | | |
| 021 | Evangelists Driver named? | | |
| 022 | Evangelists gifts/stipend agreed and treasury confirmed? | | |
| 023 | Evangelists received meeting theme? | | |
| 024 | Evangelists received nightly schedule? | | |
| 025 | Evangelists received venue details? | | |
| 026 | Evangelists received sermon topic lists? | | |
| 027 | Evangelists confirmed sermon topics and titles and sequences? | | |
| 028 | Evangelists received appeal/decision cards and confirmation regarding nights card will be used? | | |

199

# JESUS IS THE LIGHT OF THE WORLD
## Evangelistic Planning Checklist

### Preparation Checklist

| Item | Checking Questions | Answer (yes/no) | Remarks |
|---|---|---|---|
| | CAMPAIGN (EVANGELISTIC) SPEAKER continue | | |
| 029 | Evangelists confirmed happy with meeting details and plans | | |
| | MEETING SCHEDULE | | |
| 030 | Meetings Schedule draft and sent to committee leaders? | | |
| 031 | Meetings Schedule draft, including suggested amendments received from committee leaders? | | |
| 032 | Meetings Schedule completed and approved? | | |
| 033 | Committees responsible for set-up in place? | | |
| 034 | Committees responsible for nightly meeting submit schedule and confirm meeting venue ready for meeting (platform decoration, etac)? | | |
| 035 | Meeting health and safety, including risk assessment completed and clearance given by Health & Safety? | | |

# JESUS IS THE LIGHT OF THE WORLD
## Evangelistic Planning Checklist

Preparation Checklist

| Item ID | Checking Questions | Answer (yes/no) | Remarks |
|---|---|---|---|
| | **PUBLICITY** | | |
| 036 | Handbills designed? | | |
| 037 | Handbills draft received and agreed, including any adjustments? | | |
| 038 | Handbills final layout confirmed and ready to print? | | |
| 039 | Handbills print run agreed and print date confirmed? | | |
| 040 | Handbills ready for distribution? | | |
| 041 | Handbills delivered to churches? | | |
| 042 | Campaign web site designed? | | |
| 043 | Campaign web site draft approved? | | |
| 044 | Campaign web site launched? | | |
| 045 | Campaign web site updating sequence agreed? | | |
| 046 | Publicity in newspaper confirmed including payment? | | |
| 047 | Radio Publicity confirmed including costs? | | |
| 048 | Radio Publicity costs paid? | | |

# JESUS IS THE LIGHT OF THE WORLD
## Evangelistic Planning Checklist

Preparation Checklist

| Item | Checking Questions | Answer (yes/no) | Remarks |
|---|---|---|---|
| E | CAMPAIGN MANAGEMENT TEAM | | |
| 049 | Campaign Coordinator? | | |
| 050 | Campaign Assistant Coordinator 1? | | |
| 051 | Campaign Assistant Coordinator 2? | | |
| 052 | Campaign Assistant Coordinator 3? | | |
| 053 | Campaign Coordinator Elder? | | |
| F | VENUE COORDINATOR | | |
| 054 | Venue Coordinator? | | |
| 055 | Venue Assistant Coordinator 1? | | |
| 056 | Venue Assistant Coordinator 2? | | |
| G | TREASURER | | |
| 057 | Campaign Treasurer? | | |
| 058 | Campaign Assistant Treasurer 1? | | |
| 059 | Campaign Assistant Treasurer 2? | | |

# JESUS IS THE LIGHT OF THE WORLD
## Evangelistic Planning Checklist

### Preparation Checklist

| Item | Checking Questions | Answer (yes/no) | Remarks |
|---|---|---|---|
| **H** | **REGISTRATION TEAM** | | |
| 060 | Registration Coordinator? | | |
| 061 | Registration Assistant Coordinator 1? | | |
| 062 | Registration Assistant Coordinator 2? | | |
| 063 | Interest/Prospect Coordinator (s)? | | |
| **I** | **GREETING TEAM** | | |
| 064 | Head Greeter? | | |
| 065 | Assistant Head Greeter-1? | | |
| 066 | Assistant Head Greeter-2? | | |
| 067 | Greeters | | |
| **J** | **USHERS** | | |
| 068 | Head Usher? | | |
| 069 | Assistant Head Ushers? | | |
| 070 | Ushers | | |

# JESUS IS THE LIGHT OF THE WORLD
## Evangelistic Planning Checklist
### Preparation Checklist

| Item | Checking Questions | Answer (yes/no) | Remarks |
|---|---|---|---|
| **K** | **CHILDREN'S MINISTRIES TEAM** | | |
| 071 | Children Ministries Coordinator | | |
| 072 | Children Ministries Assistant Coordinators | | |
| 073 | Children Ministries voluntary staffs | | |
| **L** | **MUSIC MINISTRIES TEAM** | | |
| 074 | Music Coordinator | | |
| 075 | Assistant Music Coordinators | | |
| 076 | Musicians | | |
| 077 | Singing Evangelists | | |
| 078 | Choir/Soloists | | |
| 079 | Special Guests | | |
| **M** | **AUDIOVISUAL TEAM** | | |
| 080 | Audiovisual Coordinator | | |
| 081 | Audiovisual Assistant Coordinators | | |
| 082 | Media Operators | | |

# JESUS IS THE LIGHT OF THE WORLD
## Evangelistic Planning Checklist
Preparation Checklist

| Item | Checking Questions | Answer (yes/no) | Remarks |
|------|--------------------|-----------------|---------|
| **N** | **PRAYER WARRIORS (TEAM)** | | |
| 083 | Prayer Coordinator | | |
| 084 | Assistant Prayer Coordinators | | |
| 085 | Prayer warriors | | |
| **O** | **VISITATION TEAM** | | |
| 086 | Visitation Coordinator | | |
| 087 | Assistant Visitation Coordinators | | |
| 088 | Visitation Team members | | |
| **P** | **BIBLE WORKERS** | | |
| 089 | Bible Workers Coordinator | | |
| 090 | Assistant Bible Workers coordinators | | |
| 091 | Bible workers | | |
| **Q** | **HEALTH MINISTRIES TEAM** | | |
| 092 | Health Ministries leaders | | |
| 093 | Health Ministries members | | |

# JESUS IS THE LIGHT OF THE WORLD
## Evangelistic Planning Checklist
### Preparation Checklist

| Item | Checking Questions | Answer (yes/no) | Remarks |
|---|---|---|---|
| | ITEMS NEEDED FOR MEETINGS | | |
| 094 | Video Projector | | |
| 095 | Computers | | |
| 096 | Screens | | |
| 097 | Computer cables | | |
| 098 | Offering containers and moneybags | | |
| 099 | Cash boxes for sales | | |
| 100 | CD/DVD Duplicators | | |
| 101 | Cameras for DVD, with all cords and connections | | |
| 102 | DVD maker and CD maker for masters | | |
| 103 | Blank CD/DVD and audio cassettes to record | | |
| 104 | Response cards, Decisions and visitation cards | | |
| 105 | Bibles | | |
| 106 | Pens for people to fill out decision cards | | |
| 107 | Bible Study Lessons | | |

# Consulted Resources

Adams, Jay. Shepherding God's Flock. Grand Rapids: Zondervan, 1975.

Barna, George. Marketing the Church. Colorado Springs: Navpress, 1988.

Bounds, E. M. Power Through Prayer. Grand Rapids: Zondervan, n.d.

Bruce, A. B. The Training of the Twelve. reprint, Grand Rapids: Kregel, 1988.

Burrell, Russell. Reaping The Harvest. Fallbrook, California: Hart Books, 2007.

Eims, Leroy. The Lost Art of Disciple Making. Grand Rapids: Zondervan, Colorado Springs: Navpress, 1978.

Eims, Leroy. Disciples in Action. Colorado Springs: Navpress, and Wheaton: Victor, 1981.

European Commissions Europeaid Co-operation Office General Affairs Evaluation. Project Cycle Management Training Courses Handbook. Hassocks, West Sussex, United Kingdom: ITAD Ltd, 2001.

Finley, Mark. How to Help People Make Positive Decision. Fallbrook, California: HART Research Center.

Grenz, Stanley. A Primer on Postmodernism, Grand Rapids: Wm. B. Eerdman Publishing Co. 2001.

Hull, Bill. Jesus Christ: Disciple Maker. Old Tappan, N.J.: Revell, 1984.

Mallory, Sue and Brad Smith. The Equipping Church. Grand Rapids, Michigan: Zondervan Publishing House, 2001.

Malphurs, Aubrey. Advanced Strategic Planning: A New Model For Church and Ministry Leaders. Grand Rapids, Michigan: Baker Books, 1999.

_____. The Dynamics of Church Leadership. Grand Rapids, Michigan: Baker Books, 1990.

_____. Values-Driven Leadership: Discovery and Developing Your Core Values for Ministry. Grand Rapids, Michigan: Baker Books, 1996.

MacArthur. Faith Works: The Gospel According to the Apostles. Dallas: Word, 1993.

The MacArthur New Testament Commentary. Chicago: Moody, 1986: 94–95.

MacArthur, J., F., Jr., Mayhue, R., & Thomas, R., L. (1995). Rediscovering pastoral ministry : Shaping contemporary ministry with biblical mandates (Electronic ed.). Logos

McNamara, Carter. Field Guide To Nonprofit Strategic Planning and Facilitation. Minneapolis, Minnesota: Authenticity Consulting LLC, 2003.

_____. Field Guide to Nonprofit Program Design, Marketing and Evaluation. Minneapolis, Minnesota: Authenticity Consulting LLC, 2003.

Morgan, G. Campbell. The Gospel According to Mark. Tarrytown, N.Y.: Revell, 1927.

Pegram, R.A. "Church Growth Through Intercessory Prayer." Good News (September/October 1995) : 24.

North American Division Evangelism Institute, Eight Characteristics of a Healthy Church. http://www.nadei.org/NCD/ncd-overview.html (27 July 2004).

Robinson, Burnett. Dynamic Evangelism. Miami, Florida: Exact Printing, n.d

Sahlin, Monte. Adventist Congregations Today, New Evidence for Equipping Healthy Churches, Lincoln, NE, USA: Centre for Creative Ministry and North American Division, 2003.

Terry, John Mark. Church Evangelism. Nashville, Tennessee: Broadman & Holman Publishers, 1997.

Schwartz, Christian, and Christopher Schalk. Natural Church Development Manual. Bedford, United Kingdom: British Church Growth Association, 1985.

_____. Natural Church Development Handbook: A Practical Guide to A New Approach. Bedford, United Kingdom: British Church Growth Association, 1985.

Stalker, James. The Example of Jesus Christ. New Canaan, Conn: Keats, 1980.

Wagner, Peter C. The Healthy Church: Avoiding and Curing the 9 Diseases That Can Afflict Any Church. Ventura, California: Regal, 1996.

White, Ellen G. Evangelism. Washington, DC: Review and Herald
    Publishing Association, 1946.

_____. Testimonies to Ministers and Gospel Workers. Boise,
    Idaho: Pacific Press Publishing Association, 1962.

_____. Testimonies For The Church, vol.1. Mountain View,
    California: Pacific Press Publishing Association, 1948.

_____. Testimonies For The Church, vol. 2. Mountain View,
    California: Pacific Press Publishing Association, 1948.

_____. Christian Service. Hagerstown, MD: Review and Herald
    Publishing Association, 1947

_____. Christ's Object Lessons. Washington, D.C: Review and
    Herald Publishing Association, 1941.

Whitney, Donald S. Spiritual Disciplines for the Christian Life.
    Colorado Springs: Navpress, 1991.

Wilkins, Michael. Following the Master: Discipleship in the Steps
    of Jesus. Grand Rapids: Zondervan, 1992.